The Personality Puzzle

The Personality Puzzle

Solving the Mystery of Who You Are

José Stevens, Ph.D

JP Van Hulle

Illustrated by Lisa Locke

AFFINITY PRESS

1990

Book Design . . . . Luba Yudovich

Cover . . . . Aaron Christeaan

Technical Assistance . . . . . Lisa Mirski

Illustrations . . . . Lisa Locke

Word Processing . . . . . . M. C. Clark

Library of Congress # 89-080738
ISBN # 0-942663-06-3
Copyright # pending

To Dorothy and Edward Rose for all their guidance, love, and support.

J P Van Hulle

To my Dad, for a long life well spent.

Jose´ Stevens

CONTENTS

PREFACE

We wrote this book because we saw a profound need for a personality profile that goes beyond such concepts as abnormality and normality. From what we have observed there are no normal human beings in the population, only different kinds of people, all expressing the uniqueness of their being.

We saw the need for a personality profile that clearly addressed a person's "Essential beingness or Role", that archetypal and deep quality of self that is a personal expression of "All That Is." We have discovered that with knowledge of this role, people feel freer and more aligned with what they do best.

In this book we will show you how each person has deep within themselves six basic traits or pieces of the puzzle. We have found that from these traits people design their ambitions, their goals, their methods, and their attitudes toward life. We have designed a questionnaire, the "Essence and Personality Profile." With it you can discover your own key traits and those of your friends and loved ones.

We call the questionnaire the "Essence and Personality Profile" because we feel that it describes the basic essential quality that you are born with, and five of the primary ways that you use the personality you develop.

Clearly some people, because of the make up of their personality, have more trouble in life than others. We have accounted for these difficulties in our description of the various combinations of traits a person can have, principally in our explanation of the Obstacle. We see difficulty not as a bad thing, but as a challenge to be worked with and ultimately mastered.

We feel that the full usage of this book can release the wisdom to unlock the mysteries of your own motivations and those of the people around you. You can know what makes you who you are and what makes others who they are. This helps create understanding and understanding is a first step toward co-operation.

Here is what you will find in this book:

- A fifteen to twenty minute questionnaire with a simple code to help you determine which traits you identified with.

- A complete explanation of the key traits.

- Many photos of people depicting key traits.

- Illustrations depicting how a person would look with certain pairs of traits.

- Complete personality profiles of seven famous people and why they lived the lives they did.

CHAPTER ONE

The Essence and Personality Profile

The Essence and Personality Profile (E.P.P.) is derived from a rich body of source material that is too diverse to be mentioned here in entirety. Many of the concepts are taken from the discoveries of Gurdjieff and Ouspensky. Others are related to Jung's notion of Archetypes and to ancient Sufi knowledge of personality. Others are drawn from more conventional psychological personality theory. The E.P.P. places men and women in a larger context than the more traditional personality tests. Here we have attempted to assess qualities that are related to a person's core self in addition to behavior traits.

The E.P.P. is composed of six categories that together give a comprehensive understanding of what makes a person the way they are.

We have described the "Role" as "Essence" or that essential core quality that makes a person tick. We have designated five other categories of traits that overlay this essential role or core quality of self:

- The **Goal,** or primary motivator in life.
- The **Mode,** or method of operating to achieve that goal.
- The **Attitude,** or perspective through which all life is seen.
- The **Obstacle,** or primary stumbling block.
- The **Center,** or immediate reaction to any situation.

We believe that no other personality profile measures the key human ingredients described in the E.P.P. These ingredients are immensely helpful in assisting people to:

- accept themselves unconditionally;
- understand and target their key stumbling blocks;
- orient people to career paths and activities that they have a clear talent for;
- validate people for what they have sensed all along about themselves;
- provide invaluable information about complimentary and conflicting traits between management and employees, co-workers, couples, teachers and students, family members, friends, and acquaintances.

■■■■■■

The E.P.P.
Essence and Personality Profile

The Essence and Personality Profile (E.P.P.) is designed to give you a wide-screen overview of who you are and how you act. It attempts to assess six major characteristics that form a profile of your personality. These six characteristics are:

Goal
Mode
Attitude
Obstacle
Center
Essence Role

The qualities assessed here provide a guide for understanding your unique approach to life. Your particular style reflects and contributes to the rich variety that life has to offer. The more you know about yourself and your unique style, the more effective you become in leading a satisfying and joyful life.

You will find the personality profile on the following pages. Try to answer the questions all at one sitting during a quiet, uninterrupted time of your day. There are no right or wrong answers. It is important to tell the truth about yourself rather than trying to reply according to who you think you might like to be.

The simple scoring code can be found at the end of the profile. For each section, simply match the number of your reply with the number that corresponds to it in the code sheet. This will give you your specific qualities.

The chapters following will provide explanations and examples of each of your qualities so that you can understand what they mean and how to work with them.

Goal

The Goal is the underlying motivator in life. It is what you are always striving to accomplish, over and above your career goals and other interests.

Instructions Read over the statements below. You may see a bit of yourself in all of them. Select the *one group* of statements that most accurately describes your motivations.

1 Life looks competitive to me.
I always want to find a scenario where everyone wins; but if there is a loser it won't be me.
If things are not going my way I look for where I've lost control.

2 I want to be dedicated to a cause of great importance.
I'm most comfortable when I feel devoted.
My own needs are often of lower priority to me than those of people I love or owe loyalty to.

3 I hate criticism and am deeply wounded by rejection.
I try to accept people and situations as they are.
I would rather try to get along with others, than argue about who's "right."

4 I am very discerning about what I wear, and what I do.
I have refined or sophisticated taste, and would make a good critic.
I am an acquired taste; not friends with just anyone; and I like it that way.

5 I like to be constantly learning, experiencing things, and changing.

Just when I get my life settled, I seem to start something new.
Often I get overwhelmed, confused, and have to stop and sort things out.

6 My life seems to revolve around the same issues over and over.
I have a disability; or a significant issue in my life that affects every other part of my life on a regular basis.
My life is very simple in most respects.

7 My life is basically pleasant. Things seem to work themselves out, even if they're difficult at times.
I do not feel a big drive to accomplish anything really major during my life.
If I just relax and "go with the flow," solutions to my problems always appear.

Mode

The mode is the method of action you take to achieve your goal. This is the "how" of your general approach to life. The terms below describe many ways that you can approach tasks, people and situations.

Instructions Pick the GROUP of words that best describes your style. You may find a second and even third group that describes your style sometimes but less frequently than your main choice. These are "backup" approaches if your usual mode isn't serving the situation as well as you'd like. It's a good idea to make note of them.

1 cautious, exacting, fearful, deliberate, wary, doubtful, hesitant, thorough, tenative, discreet, careful, prudent

2 confident, powerful, important, influential, substantial, empowered, overbearing, commanding, strong, potent, authoritative, consequential

3 restrained, refined, civilized, inhibited, withheld, reserved, repressed, tasteful, cool, fastidious, well-bred, smooth

4 excited, exuberant, passionate, anticipitory, alive, involved, eager, fervent, frantic, heedless, distracted, expressive

5 persistent, disciplined, methodical, patient, repetitive, durable, tenacious, resolute, dedicated, relentless, obstinate, perservering

6 intimidating, dynamic, aggressive, assertive, pushy, risk-taking belligerent, enterprising, energetic, forceful, adventurous, ambitious

7 aware, alert, insightful, observing, attending, receptive, attentive, clear, cognizant, scrutinizing, watching, knowledgeable

Attitude

The Attitude is your perspective, and is how you view your goal as well as everything else in your life. It is the lens through which you look at the world.

Instructions First, read all the statements. You may notice that you identify with or have experienced them all. This is so for most people. Here, however, look for the one that you habitually use. Then, pick out the *group* of statements that most accurately sums up your Attitude.

1 I usually suspend judgment on what I hear until I check it out for myself.
I am suspicious of "great" new products until I have tried them out.
I frequently investigate something thoroughly before accepting it.

2 I usually focus on what should or "ought to be" done.
I constantly notice how things could be improved.
I have very high expectations of myself and others and often feel disappointed when these are not met.

3 I love to see the ultimate potential in people, things, or events.
I believe it is important to have faith, especially in hard times.
I am intrigued by and focus on achieving my dream of what *could* be.

4 People say I'm "hard to read."
I try to maintain peace and harmony, at all costs.
I can maintain a perfectly calm exterior in times of stress.

5 I easily notice what is wrong with a situation, and can play a good "devil's advocate."
Often it seems to me that nothing goes right.

I try to expect the worst; then, if something better happens, I can be pleasantly surprised.

6 I see all the facets of a situation, easily.
   I'm a very good judge of whether a task will be easy or difficult.
   I'm known for my objectivity.

7 I like to do things efficiently.
   I have a talent for seeing what will work in a situation.
   Frequently, I am frustrated by what looks to me like a clumsy or impractical approach.

Obstacle

The Obstacle is your primary stumbling block. It is your knee-jerk response to anger, frustration or difficulty. You will find a bit of yourself in all of the obstacles because most likely you have done them all from time to time. We are looking for your most instinctive reaction, however.

Instructions Select the GROUP that portrays your most typical response to the situation described below.

When I get very upset or I am under stress I tend to ...

1 have a drink, light up a cigarette, or take a drug to unwind.
   lose control or will power and do something I know I'll regret later.
   "cut off my nose to spite my face."

2 eat or drink something to fill the void I feel.
feel deprived and believe I can't have what I want
to fulfill my needs.
go shopping. Buying things makes me feel better.

3 withdraw.
feel like I'm incompetent.
blame myself for whatever went wrong.

4 internalize the problem and put barriers up.
become shy and hide behind a competent mask.
get critical or act a bit superior in defense.

5 feel trapped in my situation and helpless to get
free.
feel depressed, because there is no escape.
resent whoever manipulated me into this negative
situation.

6 become very intolerant and try to rush to a solution.
fear I'll not have enough time to get things done.
become irritated and sometimes act rashly.

7 become more determined to tough it out.
tend to become obstinate.
tune out others' feedback even if I think it might be
right.

Center

The Center determines how you will immediately react or respond in any situation. Centers energize you instantly to react in a particular manner. Of course everyone uses all three centers at times, but there is a typical reaction you have to spontaneous events. This reaction is what you look for here.

Instructions Choose the entire GROUP of statements that most applies to you.

1 I like to analyze situations.
Usually I think about a problem before doing anything about it.
I tend to think in words.
I embark on a project by thinking about it first.
If something confuses or upsets me, I need to know why.
I always try to go for the most logical solution.
I am delighted when there are clear reasons for whatever is happening.

2 I cry and laugh easily.
I tend to change moods rapidly.
I am quite perceptive and able to feel out what is needed in a situation.
I can easily imagine how someone else is feeling.
I like to express myself through music, dance and art.
I can often intuit what is happening without knowing why.
I can be very sentimental.

3 I find it hard to sit still.
When I'm in doubt I act.

I'd rather do something than talk about it.
I am competent at physical tasks.
I love the way my body feels in motion.
I like to change my job, environment or residence in order to get a fresh perspective.
I am coordinated and athletic.

Role

Your role reflects your deepest essence. However, it can be obscured by who you think you ought to be.

Here are some statements that reflect styles of *being* in the world. You may identify with more than one of them. This can be because you were conditioned in childhood to be a way that is different from who you truly are. We are looking for who you are beneath the social fabric or veneer.

It is perfectly common to be one role innately and also trained to function in another role as well. Reading about the roles in depth in Chapter Six will provide clarity as to the talents and skills you provide to society.

Instructions Circle as many statements as you closely identify with. Then go back and choose the GROUP that feels the most like you.

1 I like to work behind the scenes making sure everything runs smoothly.
Nurturing people is what inspires me most in life.
Sometimes I feel trapped into a caretaking role.
I like to quietly arrange situations to make other people happy.
I frequently perform little services that go unnoticed.

I love to take care of people and see to it they are comfortable.

I'd make someone a perfect wife or househusband.

2 I often feel a strong urge to tell people what I see is best for them.

My spiritual path is of higher importance to me than my relationships or material needs.

Sometimes I get pretty zealous in my efforts to set others on the right path.

I feel responsible for the spiritual guidance of my "flock," even if I am not a minister.

I have a natural ability to see where people are blocked and I have the urge to save them from themselves.

Compassion is the force that motivates me to relate to the world.

My friends consider me to be an inspiration to them, even if I'm not sure why.

3 I am most stimulated by inventing and remodelling.

I love to influence the mood or flavor of what's going on.

If I can't express innovative ideas I feel blocked and frustrated.

People see me as artistic and doing things with an unusual flair.

I like to invent things in my mind that have never been thought of before.

I am fascinated with how different elements combine to make a cohesive unit.

I love to create new projects from old materials.

4 I hate to have my communication misunderstood.
I love to have the last word.
I secretly (or not so secretly) love to be on stage
and to be noticed.
I often mentally correct others' communication,
whether written or verbal.
I have a little voice in my head that almost never
shuts up.
I am renowned for my wit and sense of humor.
People can't really hide the truth from me. If there
is some juicy new gossip around, I won't feel
comfortable until I've heard the details.

5 I like to get things organized.
I don't mind taking charge of situations to get
results.
The one thing that really makes me furious is an
attack on my principles—even an unwitting one.
I get so focused in one direction that I sometimes
do not see the side paths.
When people irritate me they see my sword come
out.
I will quietly but relentlessly work toward something I know is right.
I know I'm basically a strong person, and I am
quick to defend the weak and innocent.

6 I expect to be the person who is put in a leadership
position or ultimately responsible for a project.
I like to grasp the big picture and then delegate
chores to see that everything is accomplished.
I don't stop until I've really mastered what I'm
attempting.

I get frustrated if I cannot do something perfectly the first time.

I am responsible for the action flowing smoothly in whatever situation I'm in.

When things go wrong, the buck ultimately stops here.

I am only interested in "A" experiences; "A minus" is not quite enough.

7 I am innately curious and I love to study what interests me.

I am known for being objective, and I make a good mediator.

I pursue knowledge avidly.

I don't like important information to slip away unrecorded.

People value my opinion because they know that I can see any point of view objectively and fairly.

I have an inner compulsion to experiment and risk for new knowledge.

I like to research before deciding anything.

Self-Scoring Code for E.P.P.

Goal

1 Dominance – **2** Submission
3 Acceptance – **4** Discrimination
5 Growth – **6** Re-evaluation
7 Relaxation

The group you chose is your Goal in life. You will occasionally use its opposite. If you chose relaxation, you will occasionally use any one of the other goals if it makes life easier.

Mode

1 Caution – **2** Power
3 Reserve – **4** Passion
5 Perseverance – **6** Aggression
7 Observation

The group you chose is your Mode. As is the case with Goals, occasionally you will use the other one of the pair. If you chose Observation, then you will often use any of the rest of them to proceed once you've observed what approach would work best.

Attitude

1 Skeptic – 2 Idealist
3 Spiritualist – 4 Stoic
5 Cynic – 6 Realist
7 Pragmatist

The group you chose is your main Attitude in life. You will use its opposite part of the time. If you chose the neutral Attitude of Pragmatist, then you will use any attitude that it's practical to have at the moment.

Obstacle

1 Self-destruction – 2 Greed
3 Self-deprecation – 4 Arrogance
5 Martyrdom – 6 Impatience
7 Stubbornness

The Obstacle you chose is your biggest stumbling block. You will often use its opposite; but everyone experiences most if not all of the Obstacles sometimes. People in Stubbornness are particularly flexible in this one regard.

Center

Group 1 — Intellectual
Group 2 — Emotional
Group 3 — Moving

The group in which you chose the most statements is your main Center. If you chose three or more statements in another group, you most likely use that Center secondarily.

Role

1 Server
2 Priest
3 Artisan
4 Sage
5 Warrior
6 King
7 Scholar

The group that you chose indicates your Role. If you circled a number of statements in another group, then you were probably heavily conditioned by a parent of that Role.

CHAPTER TWO

How The System Works

Understanding Yourself

Now that you know your basic qualities, you can see in your day to day life that you continually act from one generalized inner motivation, using a specific style, with the same general Attitude and the same Obstacle tripping you up over and over again.

Even though you have many and various idiosyncracies, you are beginning to notice the machinery that runs you underneath your individuality. Because you are more than your machinery, you can reprogram this machine. All you need to do is to be aware of it first.

After you have read the following explanation of your key traits, alone and in combination, we suggest that you make a habit over the next few weeks of noticing when you fall into one of your habitual responses. You will notice more and more how much and on what subtle levels you have unconsciously operated from these qualities.

At that point you can start to make choices. For instance, if Stubbornness is one of your traits you can deliberately focus on being a bit more flexible next time you are upset.

Another benefit of knowing how your qualities blend together is that you will become more and more aware of your strengths. If, for instance, you discover that your primary goal is Growth, you will start to see that you are really very good at understanding new and difficult challenges. If your goal is Acceptance, you will notice how diplomatic you are and how well you can handle other people. You can use these qualities more deliberately and with the confidence that you have had them as unconscious skills all along. The more you deliberately accentuate your positive traits, the happier and more skilled you will feel. You start running your life instead of it running you.

Understanding Others

We would suggest that you also read about the traits that are not your own for purposes of recognizing them in others. It can be just as helpful to understand other people as it is to understand yourself.

Understanding other people's key traits helps you to understand who they really are. Once you see that someone is coming from a different perspective than yourself, it is easier to communicate with him in his "own language." Better communication leads to better social relations, greater acceptance, and more co-operation.

For instance, if you have a son with a goal of Acceptance and a mode of Aggression you can use his need to be liked to help him steer his boundless energy away from belligerent, aggressive behavior towards a more dynamic charisma.

If you have an employer whose attitude is Cynic and whose obstacle is Stubbornness, you will realize that he has an inner conviction that "anything that can go wrong will" and you can't convince him otherwise. Staying more realistic but flexible and showing as much efficiency as possible will endear you to this person: he will cherish your objectivity.

As you can see from these examples, the knowledge you will glean from this book can help you to notice and accept other people's limitations and strengths. You can encourage the best in those you love and with whom you work. In most cases, this knowledge will also enable you to sidestep their negative idiosyncracies.

How the Traits Relate to One Another

All traits in this book fall into one of four categories. These are Action, Expression, Inspiration, and Assimilation. The Action category includes all traits that are inherently active or involve the withholding of action. The Expression category includes all traits that are inherently expressive, creative or verbal. The Inspiration category includes all traits that are primarily related to arousal, stimulation, or the retreat from same. The Assimilation category includes all traits that are absorbtive, eclectic, and neutral.

Each goal, mode, attitude, obstacle and role has two Active traits, Expressive traits, Inspirational traits, and one Assimilative trait; making a total of 7 goals, 7 modes, etc. Of the three centers; Moving Center is the Action trait, Intellectual Center the Expressive trait, and Emotional Center the Inspirational trait.

These categories will show you how Expressive, Inspirational, Active, or Assimilative you tend to be. If your traits are clustered under one category you will use the energy of that category a great deal.

For example:

- If your traits fall mainly under the Expression category, then you will have strong expressive tendencies in your personality.
- If your traits fall mainly under the Action category, you will tend to lead a highly active life.
- If your traits fall mostly under the Inspiration category you will have a stronger tendency to feel inspired by life and be inspiring to others.
- If your traits fall mainly under the Assimilation category your personality will be very adaptive to whatever is happening around you.

If your traits are spread out over all categories, you will tend to have a balance of all of them. If you have no traits under a particular category, then you will lack tendencies in that direction.

	Inspiration		Expression		Action		Assimilation
GOAL	RE-EVALUATION	GROWTH	DISCRIMINATION	ACCEPTANCE	SUBMISSION	DOMINANCE	RELAXATION
MODE	RESERVE	PASSION	CAUTION	POWER	PERSERVERANCE	AGGRESSION	OBSERVATION
ATTITUDE	STOIC	SPIRITUALIST	SKEPTIC	IDEALIST	CYNIC	REALIST	PRAGMATIST
OBSTACLE	SELF-DEPRECATION	ARROGANCE	SELF-DESTRUCTION	GREED	MARTYRDOM	IMPATIENCE	STUBBORNNESS
CENTER	EMOTIONAL		INTELLECTUAL		MOVING		

Inspiration

Expression

Action

Assimilation

Growth and Re-evaluation—The Inspirational Goals
If you have a Goal of Growth, sometimes you will slip into Re-evaluation because there are times to move forward and there are times to consolidate.

Discrimination and Acceptance—The Expressive Goals
If you have a Goal of Acceptance, sometimes you must use Discrimination. The issue of this pair of goals is openness. If you are too open, you lose your identity and your boundaries, but if you are too closed, you can become too narrow-minded and judgmental.

Submission and Dominance—The Active Goals
If you have a Goal of Dominance, you will sometimes slide into Submission because this pair of traits is about "winning." Sometimes you want to win, but other times it is more important to you that a special cause or person wins.

Relaxation—The Assimilative Goal
If you have a Goal of Relaxation, you may use any of the goals mentioned above for variety's sake and to keep from being bored.

Reserve and Passion—The Inspirational Modes
If you have a Mode of Passion, at times you will fall into Reserve because your approach needs refining. On the other hand, if you are in Reserve Mode you will move to Passion for expansion.

Caution and Power—The Expressive Modes
If you have a mode of Power, at times you may use Caution when you need to exercise care. If you have Caution Mode you will use Power to propel you past obsessive over-concern.

Perseverance and Aggression—The Active Modes
If you have a Mode of Perseverance you will sometimes jump to Aggression to break out of a rut. Aggression will slide into Perseverance for focus and stick-to-itiveness.

Observation—The Assimilative Mode
If you have a Mode of Observation, you may at times use any of the Modes because you will have observed how you want to proceed: Cautiously, Powerfully, Reservedly, Passionately, Perseveringly or Aggressively.

Stoic and Spiritualist—The Inspirational Attitudes
If you have an Attitude of Stoic, you will use the Spiritualist Attitude at times because you want to actively pursue peace and harmony for those around you. A Spiritualist would use Stoicism to experience "inner" tranquility.

Idealist and Skeptic—The Expressive Attitudes
Sometimes you want to focus on what needs improving and sometimes you want to focus on what needs to be weeded out, depending on what you want to accomplish.

Cynic and Realist—The Active Attitudes
If you are a Cynic, you would use the Realist perspective to get a more objective point of view. If you are a Realist, you would move to Cynic to prepare yourself for a worst-case scenario.

Pragmatist—The Assimilative Attitude
If you have an Attitude of Pragmatist, you may at times take on any of the Attitudes: Stoic, Spiritualist, Cynic, Realist, Idealist, Skeptic. This is a practical thing to do. Pragmatists like to see every other point of view.

Self-Deprecation and Arrogance—The Inspirational Obstacles
If you have an Obstacle of Self-Deprecation or Arrogance, your question is one of self-worth. If your Obstacle is Arrogance, at times your illusion about your specialness will burst and you will fall into Self-Deprecation. If your Obstacle is Self-Deprecation, you will occasionally use Arrogance to drag yourself out of feeling that you have no value.

Self-Destruction and Greed—The Expressive Obstacles

If you have an Obstacle of Greed, you will at times fall into Self-Destruction because your question is, "Can I have my basic needs fulfilled?" If you are uncertain about this question, you will become greedy. You will try to grab a little more than necessary to set your fears to rest. If you can't satisfy your needs, that sense of a "bottom-less pit" augments self-destructive behavior. If you have an obstacle of Self-Destruction, you will at times use Greed to prove to yourself that you can have what you need.

Martyrdom and Impatience—The Active Obstacles

The question is power and your ability to handle things. If you have an Obstacle of Martyrdom, you will push into Impatience occasionally to try to keep from feeling like a victim of circumstance. You will want to hurry through your problems. Impatience falls into Martyrdom when circumstances seem to close in on you, such as being trapped in a traffic jam.

Stubbornness—The Assimilative Obstacle

If you have an Obtacle of Stubbornness, you may at times use any of the other Obstacles: Self-Deprecation, Arrogance, Self-Destruction, Greed, Martyrdom, and Impatience. You will act in any way that maintains the status quo.

CHAPTER THREE

How Do the Goal and Mode Work Together?

The Goal is the theme in life that you are attempting to master. The Mode is your particular method of achieving each Goal. Each combination of Goal with Mode looks different. For example, if you have a Goal of Growth, you can pursue the challenges you set up aggressively, cautiously, perseveringly, passionately, and so on. This gives your personality a certain unique flavor.

In this system the Goal is the primary motivator in your life. It is what you strive for throughout all your life and all your experiences are influenced by it. When you feel that you are achieving your Goal you feel good. When you feel that you are failing to move towards your Goal you tend to feel bad. This Goal is so basic that it colors anything you do. It is not to be confused with more limited goals such as career goals, marital goals, or the amount of money you want to make.

The Mode is the method of action you take to achieve your Goal. Everything you do is tempered by your style of action whether you approach experiences cautiously, powerfully, passionately, and so on. Although at times you may use any of them, one will characterize your *modus operandi* the most.

Next, you will find a brief description of each Goal. Following, you can read an explanation of the combination of each Goal with each Mode. All possible combinations are described. Find the combination you came up with in the questionnaire by looking for your

Goal first. Then look for your Mode and how it helps you to achieve that Goal. If you wish to, read all of them.

We've also included some stereotypical examples of people who might do very well in life having these particular key combinations.

The Goal of Growth with Corresponding Modes

You choose this Goal in life if you want to be continually challenged and presented with new and interesting material for learning. Your life tends to be quite busy as you pursue every opportunity for personal growth that you can. Good examples of people in Growth are Chuck Yeager and Amelia Earhart, who are well-known for their continual pursuit of new challenges.

At your most positive, you are continually evolving and enjoying new innovative experiences. On the negative side, you can get confused, disoriented and not know where you are going, or what you are doing with your life.

Reserve with Growth: Your life is full of new and interesting growing experiences. You don't like to be bored and you fill your busy life with elegance and tasteful surroundings. You carefully compartmentalize emotional relationships and have a few intimate friends.

Be careful not to put yourself into overwhelming, confusing situations that could cause you to become inhibited and overly withdrawn.

Examples: Confirmed bachelors, a photographer, a vintner who grows grapevines in neat rows.

Passion with Growth: Your life is full of new and interesting growing experiences. You don't like to be bored and you will stop at nothing to satisfy your need for new, fascinating lessons. You plunge in heartily where others fear to tread.

Goal: Growth

Sometimes plunging headlong into situations can cause you to catapult into confusion. A little caution may be in order.
Examples: a creative artist, an avante garde musician, a pioneer, an adventurer.

Caution with Growth: Your life is filled with new and interesting growing experiences. You feel an internal struggle between your desire to experience the new and your certainty that careful, wise planning is in order. You love to grow within a safe, solid structure like a supportive family unit or congenial work environment.

The one thing you need to be sure of is that you don't allow your fears or worries to keep you from growing.
Examples: A parish priest or minister, a monk, a traveling business-person.

Power with Growth: Your life is filled with new and interesting growing experiences. You like to know you are on top of things and in control. Your presence is always readily felt whether at home or on the job. People look to you as an authority figure and an instigator of events.

You may have no idea how overwhelming your energy can be. Be gentle with the rest of us!
Examples: an entrepreneur, the leader of an expedition, a diplomat, a photo journalist who interviews famous people.

Perseverance with Growth: Your life is filled with new and interesting growing experiences. You can't stand to be bored and you are relentless in your pursuit of every last bit of challenge you can wring from a situation. You are not above beating your head against a brick wall in your refusal to turn back or to give up.

There is such a thing as persevering too long on the trail of a lost cause. Don't fall into that trap.
Examples: People in long term relationships, social workers and therapists, caretakers of all kinds.

Passion / Growth

Aggression with Growth: Your life is filled with new and interesting growing experiences. You refuse to be bored and you focus your full, dynamic, charismatic, personality behind your pursuit of the "gusto" in life. You occasionally tend to grab situations by the throat and wrest the interesting lessons from them.

You can attract more people to support you through using your charisma than by bashing at them belligerently.

Examples: Labor union leaders, a talk show host, a campaigner, a missionary.

Observation with Growth: Your life is filled with new and interesting growing experiences. You don't like to be bored and you dislike being confused. You pursue clarity in the same manner in which you pursue vital life experiences. You are happiest when you understand who you are and where you are going and life is moving along at a rapid clip. This is a most popular combination for those with a goal of growth.

You need to remember to stay active and to participate more rather than simply observing life.

Examples: This could truly be anyone: businesspeople, teachers, housewives, etc.

The Goal of Re-evaluation With Corresponding Modes

Something you need to learn becomes a main focus of your day to day life. For example, someone with a handicap who focuses on it day in and day out might be in re-evaluation about that handicap. You may have an issue that surfaces repeatedly such as always being abandoned by the opposite sex. Or you may be a person who studies the same theme throughout your life, e.g. Jane Goodall with her all consuming research on Chimpanzees or Edsel Ford and his lifetime challenge of always being compared to his father Henry. The positive aspect of the goal of Re-evaluation is simplicity eg. taking your

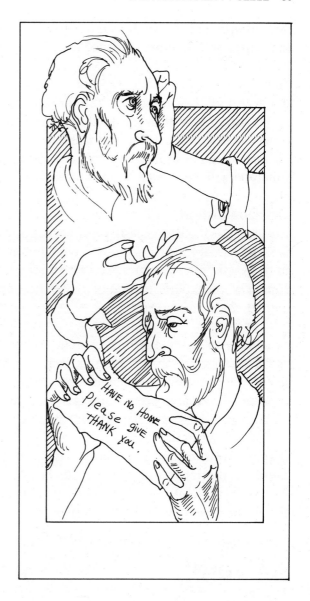

Caution / Re-Evaluation

lessons back to basics. The negative aspect is withdrawal, a kind of hiding away from what you need to examine to make your life work out.

Reserve with Re-evaluation: Your life is about looking at one or two main, basic issues that repeat regularly and you approach them with quiet dignity and in a civilized fashion. People see you as having a Victorian era flavor in your approach to life. Again and again you find yourself presented with situations in life that force you to choose a proper civilized resolution or that cause you to run away and hide instead. You may occasionally be made to feel overly conservative, brittle, or stuffy by those around you and you might wonder if everyone has forgotten what manners are. Its fine for you to be exactly who you are. Don't be forced into retreat.
Examples: an expert on manners; a careful perfectionistic gardener; a quiet, dedicated secretary.

Passion with Re-evaluation: Your life is about looking at one or two main, basic issues that show up repeatedly, but you leap fully and deeply into each new twist and representation of your main issues to wrest all possible permutations of learning from them.

You may find yourself plunging into a new hopeful situation only to find it exactly the same as the one you just left. Since the same themes will show up repeatedly until you handle them, use your depth of emotion to fully, passionately embrace the lesson to finally learn it completely
Examples: A research scientist, a mystic or religious saint, an avid collector.

Caution with Re-evaluation: Your life is about looking at one or two main, basic issues repeatedly and you proceed carefully and occasionally fearfully wanting to be absolutely sure you don't make the same mistakes that you've made in the past. You are willing to learn from your own and others' past experiences so that you can continue to examine your main lessons from continually fresh perspectives.

Goal: Re-evaluation

Take courage, for your careful approach will see you through to the appropriate end, eventually.
Examples: A hermit, a cloistered nun.

Power with Re-evaluation: Your life is about looking at one or two main, basic issues repeatedly and your life is focused on control scenarios. You are continually addressing one question: "Who is running my life?"

You can feel incredibly manipulated by fate when you find yourself in yet another problem similar to one you thought you licked. Be careful not to exhaust yourself by applying too much force to problems that need a calmer more intellectual approach.
Examples: a priest, a quadrapeligic, a miltary officer.

Perseverance with Re-evaluation: Your life is about looking at one or two main, basic issues repeatedly and you have the strength and stamina to keep repeating those lessons until you succeed. This is a most popular combination for those with Re- evaluation as a goal.

You learn quickly and easily that if you can't handle a problem the first time you run into it, a second or third try usually does it. Don't worry if it's taking you longer to get where you want to go in life than other people you know. Once you really learn a lesson you rarely forget.
Examples: A circus performer, many mentally retarded people, a concert pianist.

Aggression with Re-evaluation: Your life is about looking at one or two main, basic issues repeatedly and you tackle them with dynamic fortitude. You never give up and you let everyone know you will succeed no matter what. You get others to support you in this.

Maintain that positive attitude and you'll never have to worry about handling any problem life hands you. Your charisma is a powerful tool. Use it.
Examples: a boxer, an athlete, a marine.

Observation with Re-evaluation: Your life is about looking at one or two main, basic issues repeatedly and you attempt to observe each new facet of your lessons clearly. You, more than anyone else with this goal of re-evaluation, notice what is necessary to re-evaluate.

Your clarity is an asset because you will notice much earlier on than others with this goal that life has a pattern. Remember to stay active and to maintain a positive attitude.
Examples: Many physically disabled people; a watchful security guard; a fire lookout.

The Goal of Acceptance with Corresponding Modes

Your life is about loving and being loved. You are highly concerned with others' opinions of you and you strive to impress people favorably. In the same vein, you try to accept the situations you are in without becoming critical or judgmental. You are highly diplomatic and you know how to make others feel understood. You usually give someone who makes a mistake a second chance. Dick Van Dyke and Lucille Ball are excellent examples of individuals with the Goal of Acceptance. They are known for having "hearts of gold," in the eyes of their fans.

The positive aspect of the Goal of Acceptance is the ability to experience unconditional love. The negative side is ingratiation or bending too far in order to please.

Reserve with Acceptance: In order to be the friendly person you want to be, you share your good taste and refinement with others. People know they can count on your high quality, organized and mannerly approach to put them at ease in any situation. Internally, however, you may have difficulty being as accepting of yourself in undignified moments as others would be of you.
Examples: a professional host or hostess, an office manager.

Goal: Acceptance

Passion with Acceptance: In order to be the friendly person you want to be, you go out of your way to be warm and accepting. You passionately collect people, pets, appliances; anything that intrigues you. Your life is brimming full of people and things to play with. You have a pretty healthy opinion of yourself; however, you have to watch out for over empathizing with other peoples dramas. This is a popular combination for those with a goal of acceptance.
Examples: a bartender, owner of a tavern, an adventurer, children's storyteller.

Caution with Acceptance: In order to be the friendly person you want to be, you carefully choose a few close intimates whom you allow to touch your life deeply. It takes you quite a while to let people into your heart but once they are firmly ensconced there, you are everlastingly loyal. You have a tendency to be much too hard on yourself.
Examples: a diplomat, a college professor, could be almost anyone.

Power with Acceptance: In order to be the friendly person you want to be, you are willing to be a leader, mentor, and confidant to others. You use all the strength and capability that is continually at your fingertips to make others feel secure and comfortable. You may have difficulty accepting yourself if life seems out of control momentarily. Give yourself a break.
Examples: an executive, a priest or minister, a lawyer, a physician.

Perseverance with Acceptance: In order to be the friendly person you want to be, you are always willing to pitch in wherever necessary to help your friends and neighbors raise the barn, fix the car, or move from one house to another. You are an unswervingly loyal buddy and are willing to support people only at the level they can handle at the present moment. You have a tendency to persevere in lost causes, however, and attempt for years to make an impossible situation better. You need to be appreciated to recognize your own worth.
Examples: a doctor, a carpenter, a social worker.

Aggression / Acceptance

Aggression with Acceptance: In order to be the friendly person you want to be, you approach people boisterously and with overwhelming energy. You can charismatically enroll them in your latest wild adventure or belligerently berate them if they misbehave. You tend to keep a pretty steady and positive opinion of yourself unless you feel you have made a poor judgement. Then you attack yourself unnecessarily. Be kind to yourself.
Examples: a logger, a warehouse man, a pilot, a circus clown.

Observation with Acceptance: In order to be the friendly person you want to be, you look for ways to fit appropriately into the lives of those you love. You are very clear about just when a word of encouragement is needed or when you need to value someone's privacy. You continually watch for what is needed. You tend to self-examine a lot and therefore see all your own human frailities. Try to stay as objective about yourself as you are about others.
Examples: an executive secretary, a teacher, a psychotherapist.

The Goal of Discrimination with Corresponding Modes

Your life is about selective, fine tuned, critical judgement. You appreciate precision and your focus tends to be on getting rid of what isn't up to your standards. There are two types of discriminators: Those who tend to be exceedingly picky and rejecting and those who turn their critical faculties toward sophistication. A rejecting discriminator is very fault-finding and has a hard time making friends. In extreme cases, he may even reject society entirely. A sophisticated discriminator is often a gourmet, a connoisseur, and a patron of fine arts. William F. Buckley is a fine example of this latter type.

The positive aspect of the Goal of Discrimination is sophistication, that is, choosing only what one deems best. The negative aspect is rejection.

Goal: Discrimination

Reserve with Discrimination: In your attempt to select only the finest you approach the task with elegance and refinement. You value restraint and are considered a very civilized, sophisticated individual. This is a popular combination for those with a goal of discrimination.
Examples: A British butler, an interior decorator, a wine critic, a maitre d'.

Passion with Discrimination: In your attempt to select only the finest you fervently strive to examine life to the fullest with incisive intensity. You may passionately embrace or reject friends, cohorts, and situations you are in contact with and often you leave people nervously unsettled as to where they fit in your scenario.
Examples: a professional critic, a spokesperson for a perfume company or representative of a Rolls Royce dealership, a beautician.

Caution with Discrimination: In your attempt to select only the finest you carefully and slowly pick through your options. You can feel an internal tension between the desire to move forward by picking and choosing the appropriate path and the need to proceed very cautiously.
Examples: A munitions expert, an explosives manufacturer, a surgeon, an expert watch repairman, a jeweler.

Power with Discrimination: In your attempt to select only the finest you wrest control of every possible scenario so as to mold it to your specifications. People can find you overpowering though admiring your forceful presentation. You always project a strong, powerful image.
Examples: A television commentator, a multi-national corporation executive, a bishop or church leader.

Perseverance with Discrimination: In your attempt to select only the finest you leave no stoned unturned. You search relentlessly for the best relationship, products, and environments. You are never happy with less than perfection but nevertheless can remain immutably engaged in attempting to improve a less than perfect situation. *Examples*: a reviewer, a products tester, a quality control expert, a buyer for a top fashion clothes outlet, a hairdresser.

Aggression with Discrimination: In your attempt to select only the finest you are willing to push yourself and others to the limit. You have a strong personal charisma and dynamism that thrusts you to the forefront in whatever you undertake. However you are also often willing to force people and situations into your idea of what is correct. You have to guard against becoming insulting or belligerent if things don't go immediately your way.
Examples: Professional athlete, coach, Olympic champion, race car driver.

Observation with Discrimination: In your attempt to select only the finest you look thoroughly and keenly into each opportunity that life provides. You are willing to educate yourself to discover and appreciate the best quality wines, fashions, products, educational facilities, and so forth. People consider you a connoisseur.
Examples: wine critic, literary reviewer, theater critic.

The Goal of Dominance with Corresponding Modes

Your life is about control. You see things in light of winning or losing and you always want to be on the winning side. You want others whom you admire, love, and respect to win also. You will be happier if you look at life from the "win-win" perspective rather than from the "win-lose," competitive viewpoint. Good examples of people

Reserve / Discrimination

with the goal of dominance are Eleanor Roosevelt, Queen Elizabeth I of England and Henry Ford.

The positve aspect of having the goal of dominance is good leadership skills. The negative aspect is bullying people into win/lose situations.

Reserve with Dominance: When an opportunity to lead arises, you step smoothly, tactfully, and subtly to the fore. You make a perfect diplomat. People admire your control and your sense of order. At times you may experience a conflict between your desire to lead and your repressed, inhibited side.
Examples: diplomat, symphony conductor, editor.

Passion with Dominance: When an opportunity to lead arises, you plunge happily into the challenge. Many people use you as a mentor or guide. They are sure you know the right path and can direct them to it. You tend to be cheerfully optimistic about your capabilities and rightfully so. You may overwhelm people with your well meaning programs for them and you have to be wary of becoming overly wrapped up in your busy activities.
Examples: A therapist, a salesperson, an advertising executive.

Caution with Dominance: When an opportunity to lead arises, you use tried-and-true methods to achieve success. You control best from a mainstream position and tend to be conservative. You can have a great internal conflict between the part of you that wants to plunge ahead into control and the equally strong part of you that wants you to be careful and cautious.
Examples: A medical researcher, an Internal Revenue Service employee, a budget director.

Power with Dominance: When an opportunity to lead arises, you take control with full authority and with a strong sense of your own power and commitment. You are a recognizable force in the world and you are almost always enormously successful in whatever

Goal: Dominance

career path you choose. You can only be hindered if you alienate your loyal followers by being too demanding and dictatorial. This is a popular combination for those with a goal of dominance.
Example: A corporate leader, an entrerpeneur, a world leader.

Perseverance with Dominance: When an opportunity to lead arises, you grab the bit in your teeth and pursue your ends with headstrong focus. You hate to give up, since giving up feels like losing to you. You can be a good leader if you encourage yourself to be more flexible and more understanding of other peoples' needs.
Example: a bureaucrat, an author, a heart surgeon, a corporate lawyer.

Aggression with Dominance: When an opportunity to lead arises, you charm your way into the limelight. Once there, you are dynamically, energetically, even belligerently in control. The iron hand in the velvet glove becomes apparent. You are tempted to wrest control of a situation from those you deem incompetent. You need to temper your dominance with compassion.
Example: a boxer or any professional athlete, an upscale executive.

Observation with Dominance: When an opportunity to lead arises, you present yourself as the clear and logical choice for the position. You are willing to do your homework to create a winning situation for all concerned. You watch carefully for opportunities to lead so that you can step in and save the sinking ship. Be careful not to fall down in the empathy department. Not everyone is as focused and clear as you are.
Example: A building contractor, an architect, an administrative assistant, a small business owner.

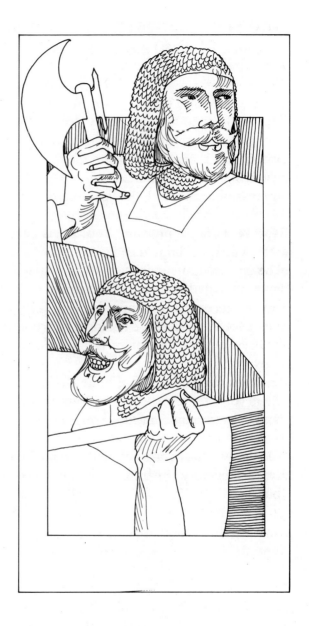

Observation/ Dominance

The Goal of Submission with Corresponding Modes

You dedicate and devote yourself to causes greater than yourself. You are devoted to your family, friends, and beliefs. You need to remember to include yourself in the picture. Ralph Nader is a good example of a person with the Goal of Submission, dedicated to protecting the consumer. Another person with an obvious Goal of Submission was the Noble Peace prize winner, Mother Theresa.

Reserve with Submission: Your life is about putting the needs of others you care about ahead of your own and you have a strict code of behavior within which you allow yourself to operate You temper devotion with dignity and don't usually allow yourself to be overly sentimental or mushy; however, your feelings run deep. You need to let people see the love behind your cool reserve.
Examples: housewife, nun, priest, monk.

Passion with Submission: Your life is about putting the needs of others you care about ahead of your own and you fervently pursue those causes you believe in. You are a perfect promoter and could easily get someone whom you feel is worthy elected president. You hold very strong beliefs and will uphold them to the maximum. You can become very frustrated if you have not yet discovered causes you can truly believe in. Look for those causes. This combination is a favorite for those with a goal of submission.
Examples: Campaign manager, leader of reform movement, mystic or saint.

Caution with Submission: Your life is about putting the needs of others you care about ahead of your own and you are very concerned about doing that correctly. You are a careful, quiet person and sometimes you need to make sure that your voice is heard and that you are not taken for granted. As long as you feel loved you can put

Goal: Submission

up with almost anything. You take very good care of those whom you love.

Examples: Doctor, nurse, aide, nursery maid, attendant for disabled person.

Power with Submission: Your life is about putting the needs of others you care about ahead of your own and you will overcome any obstacle in your path to that end. You are a strong person and you powerfully communicate your dedication to your cause or people. You can be a very inspiring speaker or proponent for higher ideals. You need to realize that others may not always be as involved in those causes as you are.

Examples: Political environmentalist, leader of a reform movement, Proponent for or against an issue, for example, gun control.

Perseverance with Submission: Your life is about putting the needs of others you care about ahead of your own and you are unswerving in your continued devotion. Once you have given your loyalty to someone or something you rarely change your mind. It is hard for you to notice a lost cause and you can spend an endless amount of time pursuing inappropriate ends if you are not careful. If you make good choices about a mate, family, and/or career you can be a perfectly happy person. This combination is a favorite for those with a goal of submission.

Examples: Clergy, career employee, mother of ten.

Aggression with Submission: Your life is about putting the needs of others you care about ahead of your own and you boldly proclaim yourself the defender of those people or causes. You can be as dangerous as a mother bear defending her cubs. People want you on their side because of your charisma, dynamism, and loyalty. Watch your temper.

Examples: Union leader, military sergeant, religious zealot.

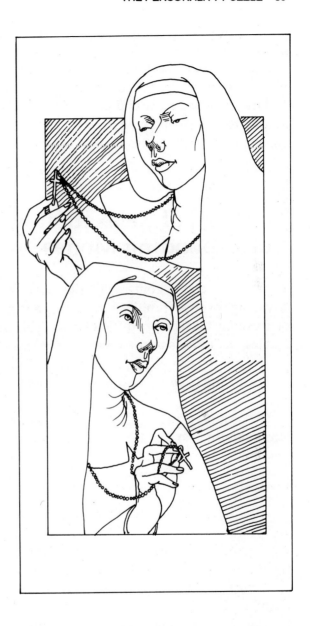

Reserve / Submission

Observation with Submission: Your life is about putting the needs of others you care about ahead of your own and you spend a lot of your time looking for those little ways to be really supportive. You like to observe the true needs of those people and causes you support and fulfill them quietly and perfectly. You have to be careful to get around to pampering yourself for a change.
Examples: Valet, head waiter, secretary.

The Goal of Relaxation with Corresponding Modes

Your life is about going with the flow. Your lesson is to take advantage of opportunities as they arise and not overwhelm them or deliberately take a more difficult path. This path is more about rest and less about resistance to events, people, and situations in life. Be careful not to become apathetic or inert. Princess Grace of Monaco and Nat King Cole are examples of people with the goal of relaxation.

The positive aspect of relaxation is to be free-flowing and flexible, while offering no resistance to what life serves up. The negative possibility is to be stuck in resistance to life's lessons and experiences.

Reserve with Relaxation: You want your life to proceed smoothly and you amble through it with a quiet, dignified step. You appreciate elegant, luxurious surroundings and you usually arrange to have them provided for you. You are an expert at those small details of etiquette that make people comfortable. You give an excellent tea party. If you are not careful you could experience less intimacy in relationships than others do and you may regret this later in life.
Examples: Hostess, interior decorator, etiquette advisor.

Goal: Relaxation

Passion with Relaxation: You want your life to proceed smoothly and in that process you want to investigate many areas of talent and skill. You tend to embrace many hobbies, crafts, and pursue unusual people for entertainment. You have an unfortunate tendency to rush about in an uneven fashion. It is hard for you to keep from struggling upstream against the normal flow of your life.
Examples: An avid sport fan, a patron of the arts, a dilettante.

Caution with Relaxation: You want your life to proceed smoothly and in that process you refuse to rock the boat. You would rather let life come to you rather than to wear yourself ragged trying to look for it. You like the status quo and settle down to a comfortable rut quite easily. You need to be sure you don't let life pass you by altogether. Shake yourself up a bit occasionally, and try something new.
Examples: A retail clerk, a franchise restaurant owner.

Power with Relaxation: You want your life to proceed smoothly and you arrange for that in an organized, capable fashion. "Smooth but not boring" is your motto. You are like an idling engine, extremely powerful but not necessarily in pursuit of anything. You make an excellent role model for how to be a "generically empowered individual." You can get frustrated if you allow too many demands on your strength or if you allow life to get a little too stagnant.
Examples: A daycare center operator, a schoolteacher, a good host or hostess.

Perseverance with Relaxation: You want your life to proceed smoothly and you are always in movement. You enjoy change as long as it is slow, steady, continual, and revealing. You allow life to flow into place around you with very little orchestration on your part. Stubbornness and resistance could be your downfall.
Examples: flight attendant, train engineer, computer operator.

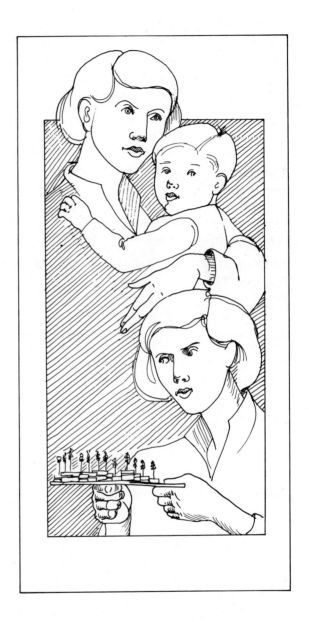

Power / Relaxation

Aggression with Relaxation: You want your life to proceed smoothly but you also like it spicy. If the opportunity for excitement arises you'll pursue that path over any other more sensible one. You easily charm others into getting your basic needs met. You need to be careful not to leave a trail of broken hearts behind you.

Examples: A gigolo, a high-priced call girl, a gambler, a groupie.

Observation with Relaxation: You want your life to proceed smoothly and you are willing to study the opportunities that arise in order to choose the smoothest, most pleasant path for yourself. You grasp the concept of "surrender being a valuable challenge" rather than something to be avoided. You will only have difficulty if you struggle. Relax.

Examples: A therapist, a director of activities on a cruise ship, a restaurant owner.

Mode: Reserve

Mode: Caution

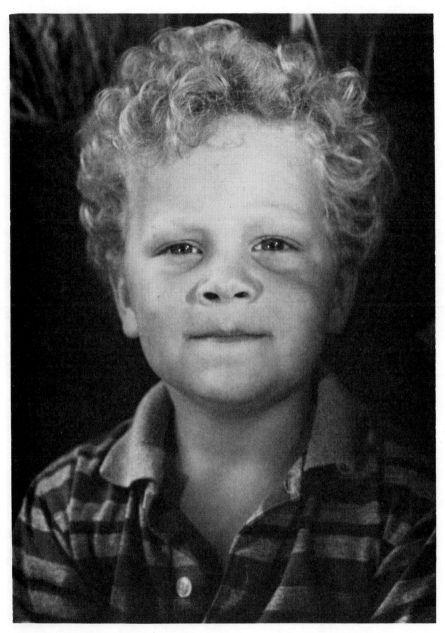

Mode: Power

Mode: Perserverance

Mode: Aggression

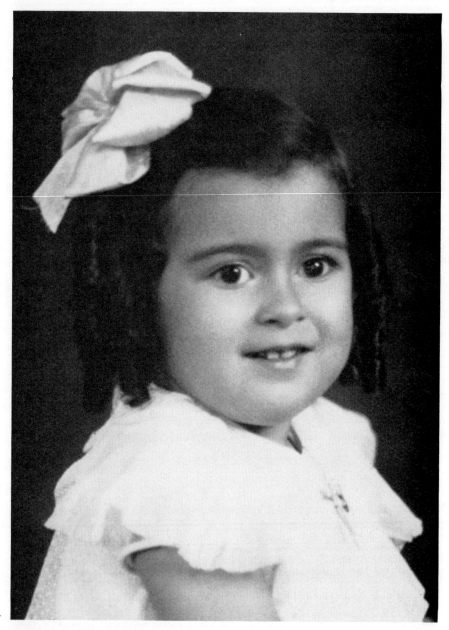

Mode: Observation

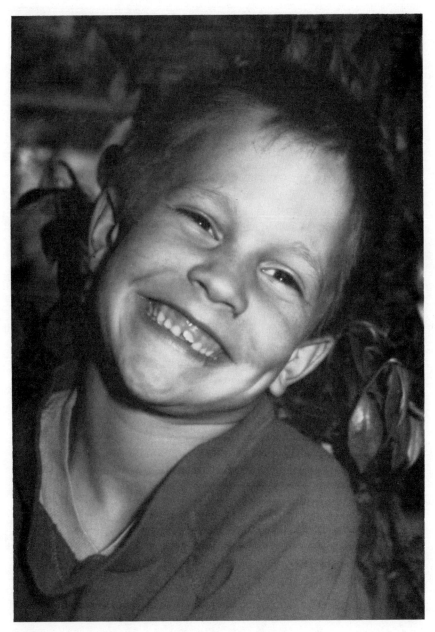

Mode: Passion

CHAPTER FOUR

How Your Attitude Works with Your Obstacle

The Obstacle is your major stumbling block throughout your life.

Your Attitude is your primary perspective in life. It is the lens through which you look at the world. Each Attitude has a positive and a negative side. Being positive tends to make life easier and you won't feel as much need to fall into your Obstacle. Being negative makes life unpleasant and tends to make you stumble over your Obstacle.

Your Obstacle is your primary stumbling block. It is how you generally behave at your worst. It tends to block efforts to reach your Goal and is a response always based on fear. Operating out of your Obstacle tends to make you and others dealing with you, miserable. Unlike your Attitude and the other traits described in this book, it is best to try to eliminate your Obstacle entirely.

Next, you will find a description of each Attitude followed by an explanation of how each Attitude and Obstacle impact each other. There are forty-nine combinations in all, only one of which will apply primarily to you. Your Attitude is the key to eliminating your Obstacle.

First find your Attitude and then see how your Obstacle interacts with it.

The Stoic Attitude with Corresponding Obstacles

The way you view the world is with outward calm and neutrality. You are stable in a crisis because you can align yourself with whatever is happening. You value peace and tranquility above more extreme forms of expression. You must be careful not to give up in the face of adversity in order to keep the peace.

Stoic with Self-Deprecation: Whenever life looks negative, you are certain that you are to blame somehow, and you become quiet and self effacing. You immediately cover your feelings with a blank demeanor while your insides are in a turmoil trying to resolve the problem. Your biggest fear is that everything that goes wrong in your world is your fault. This is simply not true. It is your illusion. You could achieve tranquility much more quickly if you would be willing to allow others to aid you in resolving your problem rather than wallowing in self blame. Give yourself a break.

Stoic with Arrogance: Whenever life looks negative, you retreat into an icy, superior-looking demeanor. You may feel quite critical and judgmental of others at these moments, wanting to lay the blame at the doorstep of anyone but yourself. On the other hand, you may merely be embarrassed or feel shy and nervous about your "slip showing." Nevertheless, you still tend to look snobby and superior or cold and removed to others. They still feel judged by you or are uncomfortable around you in these moments.

Your biggest fear is "being judged" but you would do anything in your power to mask that vulnerability. The most freeing path in this case is to look at the situation from a larger context with a sprinkling of humor.

Stoic with Self-Destruction: Whenever life looks negative, you are truly sitting on a powder keg. You have a tendency to develop strongly self-destructive habits such as "substance abuse" while

Attitude: Stoic

maintaining an outwardly calm and competent face to show the world. Other people rarely hear your cries for help because you keep your expression internalized and you do not look like you are in trouble.

Your biggest fear is that life is not worth living and that all the effort you've put into it so far is pointless. You need to face reality. You may have a bad habit but your life is worth living. Think about arranging a supportive group such as Alcoholics Anonymous or a therapy group to hammer down some of those walls you've built up between yourself and others.

Stoic with Greed: Whenever life looks negative, you seek to fill the void by burying yourself in consumable luxuries. You may eat a whole cheesecake, drink a bottle of Jack Daniels, or go on a credit card shopping spree. You have a great stake in seeming unruffled and in control, even while these vastly out-of-control urges overtake you. This leads to a discordant internal state in which you attempt to "buy peace and happiness" but know you cannot. You also have a tendency to drop out of sight and be completely out of reach of all your friends during periods of emotional turmoil.

Your biggest fear is that there is not enough to go around. You must learn to look within yourself for your satisfaction, instead of seeking it outwardly in goods or in others' attention.

Stoic with Martyrdom: Whenever life looks negative you have a quiet inner conviction that you are being picked on and that somehow you have become a victim of circumstances. The feeling of being trapped throws off that inner sense of peace that you value so highly. It is quite easy for you to get into a resigned, despairing state wherein improvement looks hopeless.

Your greatest fear is that of being used and unappreciated. You may need a neutral outsider's perspective to enable you to see more choices and therefore more creative solutions to what you feel are hopeless situations. You deserve to be appreciated, and you probably are, without your notice.

Stoic / Arrogance

Stoic with Impatience: Whenever life looks negative, you can become incredibly frustrated. You feel ripped between your true need for peace and tranquility and your impatient desire to get that problem handled now. All of this goes on behind the mask of "calm competency" you wear. Your frustration may even build to a bursting point wherein you may shock and surprise those around you who are accustomed to your usual even temper.

Your greatest fear is that you will not "get it all done" or handled. You need to see that there is an abundance of time in your life to handle anything important. You also need to discover places to let off steam.

Stoic with Stubbornness: Whenever life looks negative you dig your heels in and become totally implacable. Confronting you at this point is like confronting a brick wall. It doesn't move. When people approach you, when you are in this state, they don't know what to do: you look totally unreadable.

Your biggest fear is losing control. You need to allow changes to take place slowly and logically so that you have time to adjust to necessary shifts without feeling threatened.

The Spiritualist Attitude with Corresponding Obstacles

The way you view the world is as a vast canvas of possibilities. You can easily conceive of all the possibilities that a situation ultimately has to offer. You are much more interested in what "could be" achieved in life rather than what has already been accomplished. You live so much in potentials that if you're not careful you can lose track of day to day reality.

Spiritualist with Self-Deprecation: When life looks negative, you experience a great swing from your usually very expanded state into a small constricted "I am worthless" state. You can become extremely illogical in your negative self-evaluation. You believe that

Attitude: Spiritualist

you are totally at fault for anything negative, no matter how inaccurate that viewpoint might appear to others.

Your biggest fear is that somehow you are at fault for anything negative that happens in your world. You need an injection of logic and objectivity from a source you can trust. This will put you back on track to being your usually happy, optimistic self.

Spiritualist with Arrogance: When life looks negative, you immediately start to look for whatever external person or situation caused the problem. Your natural tendency would be to assume that you couldn't possibly be at fault. You tend to view others as potentially good and useful; but subtly, or even blatantly, inferior to yourself. Nevertheless, you tend to be friendly and outgoing and often unconscious of your superior airs.

Your greatest fear is being misunderstood and undervalued. You need to take more responsibility for the situations in which you find yourself. You arranged them more often than you know, even the negative scenarios.

Spiritualist with Self-Destruction: When life looks negative, all of your optimistic enthusiasm for life is snuffed out. You feel deflated and believe that life is hardly worth living. If your dreams can't come true, you'd just as soon leave the game altogether. You try to control this deflation with death-defying thrills and stunts, such as driving at 100 mph in a convertible with no seat belt on. These thrills, of course, are transitory and may lead to an untimely death.

Your greatest fear is that dreams can never be realized. You need to recognize that life is not so black-and-white and start creating a more realistic viewpoint.

Spiritualist with Greed: When things look negative, you tend to go on a wild spree of excess to make yourself feel better. You don't like to look at what is going wrong; you'd rather immerse yourself in a whirlwind of activity, shopping sprees, parties, or socializing to distract yourself. You may have a tendency in times of extreme stress to turn to alcohol or cocaine.

Spiritualist / Impatience

Your greatest fear is having to confront some extraordinarily negative truth. You need support in facing your problems squarely and truthfully at an early stage before they become impossible to control.

Spiritualist with Martyrdom: When life looks negative, you begin to feel constricted, trapped, and despairing of ever being able to fulfill your dreams. Your normally optimistic spirit feels like whimpering in its distress. You feel boxed in by circumstances beyond your control.

Your greatest fear is that there is no release that will get you back into the world of possibilities that you usually enjoy. You need training to catch the warning signs that would tell you that you are heading into another closed box. You also need to be willing to aggressively break those chains that bind you by standing up for yourself, even if it means getting angry.

Spiritualist with Impatience: When life looks negative, you rush about madly trying to cover all angles at once. In your haste to solve the problem, you throw dozens of ineffective or slightly effective solutions into its path, meanwhile pretending to yourself that everything is probably just fine. The frantic demeanor you adopt tends to scare away many of your would-be supporters.

Your greatest fear is that no matter how much energy you throw into solutions your problem will still be insurmountable. You need to slow down, think calmly, and use a little more logic.

Spiritualist with Stubbornness: When life gets negative, you tend to immediately deny the problem and often refuse to look at it. You can even become highly irritated if those close to you continue to bring up the fact that there is a problem. You don't like to have your optimistic view of the world threatened.

Your greatest fear is that the rosy picture of life that you hold is not so rosy, and that you will not be able to control that. You need to realize that having problems is a natural and normal part of life that need not destroy your world view. You are strong enough to conquer anything if you will just face it.

The Skeptic Attitude with Corresponding Obstacles

The way you view the world encompasses many layers of perspective. You take nothing at face value but need to investigate all of the many facets of whatever situation is presented to you. Then you decide what you believe about it. You are excellent at investigating but need to avoid becoming overly suspicious.

Skeptic with Self-Deprecation: When life looks negative, you not only become certain that there is a flaw in the situation, but also that you are somehow the cause. When something goes wrong, you go over and over what you should have done. You tend to attack yourself unmercifully at these times.

Your biggest fear is that you are certainly to blame for the problems and that everyone will blame you forever for not having prevented them from arising. You need to realize that hindsight is always easier than foresight. Be gentle with yourself. Blaming yourself is useless. Put your energy into more careful planning instead of looking backward.

Skeptic with Arrogance: When life looks negative, you tend to judge and blame others mercilessly for what they did wrong. Depending on your personal style, you may be loud and vicious about this or quietly condemning. Either way it makes others so uncomfortable that they would really rather not be around you at these times. When you turn this judgment against yourself, you really suffer.

Your greatest fear is that some idiot will do something terribly destructive that you can't rectify, but whose consequences you will have to live with. You need to see that blaming someone is not always as cut and dried as it may appear. You need to feel more confident and less threatened. You have more control than you think and blame is not always that easy to assign.

Attitude: All Skeptics

Skeptic with Self-Destruction: When life looks negative, you tend to notice element after element of the problem, until you are so certain that life is nothing but problems that you begin to rip yourself apart over it. Since all of life seems to be part of the problem at this point, you can become suicidal or you can cloud over this agonizing viewpoint in alcohol or drugs.

Your biggest fear is that there is nothing positive you can discover that would make life worth living. You need to apply your strong investigative talents toward uncovering positive, meaningful threads in your life.

Skeptic with Greed: When life looks negative, you attempt to appease the angry side of yourself with goodies. A new dress or a bouquet of flowers can cheer you up and counterbalance your negative viewpoint.

Your biggest fear is that there will be no good coming in to balance the bad and you will end up with nothing. You need to get a handle on your occasional compulsive excesses. You don't have to run so hard from the negative. It can be easier to face than you think.

Skeptic with Martyrdom: When life looks negative, you feel trapped and certain that there is no way out of your dilemma. You often feel that someone or something has done it to you. You are suspicious of any alternatives or possibilities that could set you free; you are also certain at this point that you are unappreciated.

Your biggest fear is that you will be totally unappreciated and trapped in your problems. You need to investigate further ways that you can help yourself and not feel so pushed around by others.

Skeptic with Impatience: When life looks negative, you feel frustrated, prickly, and judgmental. The problem often looks intolerable or irritating and you just want to push the whole situation and the people involved in it out of your focus. It is hard for you to take the time to investigate properly at these times, and you tend to remain in a chronic doubting state.

Your biggest fear is that your problems will be so unwieldy that

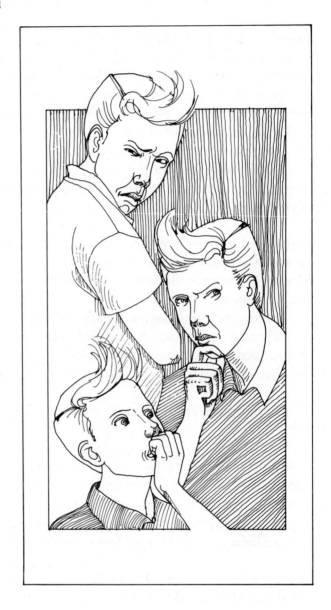

Skeptic / Stubbornness

you won't have enough time or energy to solve them correctly. You need to slow down, become less frenetic and use your strong investigative strengths to logically seek out the best solutions.

Skeptic with Stubbornness: When life looks negative, you refuse to move from your doubting position until all your questions are set to rest. You are determined to uncover every possible facet of the situation thoroughly before you decide what to do. You may appear quite suspicious to others and they can find you unmoveable and tiresome at these times.

Your greatest fear is that your problems will career out of your control before you can figure out how to handle them. You need to be more flexible and to realize that many problems can be solved without such a thorough investigation. Use your perceptivity.

The Idealist Attitude with Corresponding Obstacles

The way you view the world leads you into a constant state of change. You are always letting go of the present and anticipating the next experience. You are rarely satisfied with the status quo and are constantly searching for ways to improve a situation. You often tend to see things as being better than they are and can be very disappointed when reality strikes home. You have a natural talent for improving any experience; however, you can be surprisingly naive.

Idealist with Self-Deprecation: When life looks negative, you lose faith in your abilities. You are sure that your generally reliable talent for making things run smoothly has failed and therefore you must be to blame for anything that goes wrong. You can feel so crushed by this that you stop looking for a solution temporarily.

Your greatest fear is that you can never live up to your own standards and you, therefore, have no worth. You need to focus and be proud of what you have already accomplished while tempering

Attitude: Idealist

your idealism with more reality. Self-deprecation with idealism is a common combination.

Idealist with Arrogance: When life looks negative, you can become extremely critical towards anyone who is not in alignment with your idealistic views. You may even blame them for being the problem. On the other hand, you may react to difficulty by internalizing the problem and becoming extremely shy, self-conscious, embarrassed, and even tongue-tied when you are not living up to your expectations.

Your greatest fear is being judged about not meeting your own ideals. You need to realize that the opinions of others are not necessarily correct or paramount and release yourself and them from blame. You do not have to be perfect all the time.

Idealist with Self-Destruction: When life looks negative, you have a tendency to have unrealistic expectations that there could be an easy way out through your difficulties. You have a tendency to grab a drug or alcohol or bury yourself in some other distraction to keep from facing what looks to be an impossible problem. The way you handle difficulty is to steadfastly refuse to look at it.

Your greatest fear is that life is not worth living if you cannot have your ideal picture; and you are sure you cannot have it. You need to admit your problems and then notice that ideal situations can be achieved but in time and with considerable effort.

Idealist with Greed: When life looks negative, you want to shop, eat, or somehow alter your situation because you believe that this will shift the problem as well. You may have great difficulty with your weight because it is so easy to eat, to shift into a more pleasant state. In addition to, or instead of, food you may rely on cigarettes, alcohol, or other crutches to give you quick, pleasurable mood-alteration. These bad habits are hard to break because so often they do help you get a better handle on your problem, for a short while.

Your biggest fear is that you will be unable to alter your state easily and thus be overwhelmed by your difficulties. You need to pacify that need for a quick fix with something positive, like a good

Idealist / Greed

talk with a friend, a meditation practice, gardening or exercise. After you feel protected, you can look at your problems without such fear.

Idealist with Martyrdom: When life looks negative, you often feel trapped in a much worse scenario than you would have expected. You feel you should be able to handle this but, on the other hand, you feel victimized by people or circumstances outside your control. The more you struggle, the more you second-guess yourself. Your idealism makes it difficult for you to drop your feeling of martyrdom.

Your biggest fear is that you are trapped in a hopeless situation that somehow you should have anticipated but did not. You need to investigate your options more clearly and more fully. You are never really trapped in a box with no way out. You just have not seen the solution yet. Don't waste time with "should haves."

Idealist with Impatience: When life looks negative, you rush about madly attempting to find the perfect solution. You can become highly intolerant of anything or anyone that hinders your movement at these times and little irrelevant things can irritate you.

Your greatest fear is that there won't be enough time to get your life into perfect working order. You need to calm down and be more gentle with your friends and loved ones. You need to learn to be satisfied with your life the way it is today and stop anticipating how much better it could be later. The future can take care of itself. You only have to live through one day at a time.

Idealist with Stubbornness: When life looks negative, you have a tendency to apply solutions to the problem that you think should work because they have in the past. These solutions may be useless in the present situation but, nevertheless, you can be quite obstinate in your efforts to make them fit. You hang onto ideal pictures with great determination. This can keep you from seeing reality and, therefore, being able to solve your problems.

Your greatest fear is that your problems are out of control and you are heading for severe disappointment. You need to be more flexible in your search for solutions and you especially need to see that there can be more than one ideal solution.

The Cynic Attitude with Corresponding Obstacles

The way you view the world is to anticipate all the possible problems that could arise in life so that you are then able to prepare for them or avoid them. You often take a devil's advocate position and your friends can therefore find you contradictory and difficult. You can wear people down with your pessimism and drive them away without ever realizing it. Your Attitude keeps you protected from negative surprises, however, and that makes you feel more comfortable. You need to avoid becoming overly negative or condemning.

Cynic with Self-Deprecation: When life looks negative, you immediately become quite self-condemning. You are certain that you should have anticipated this difficulty and avoided it. Even so, your viewpoint that "anything that can go wrong, will go wrong" has been reinforced. With this attitude, you can engender incredible self-hatred.

Your greatest fear is that in the face of inevitable catastrophe you will be unprepared and fail to find a solution. This makes you almost poison yourself with anger. You need to have a more realistic and objective viewpoint. This is so difficult for you to achieve on your own, we recommend a professional support person in times of great stress.

Cynic with Arrogance: When life looks negative, you cannot resist saying, "I told you so" to others. You believe that others in their ignorance have failed to see what you have seen all along. You are very good at anticipating negative scenarios and avoiding them and you have little respect for those who do not. You especially become

Attitude: Cynic

irritated if you are then drawn into a problem that others have created.

Your greatest fear is that everything in life will turn out badly, probably due to "some moron" you have no control over. You need to be less critical. Others are less flawed and more human than you would imagine. Life is not nearly as negative as you tend to believe.

Cynic with Self-Destruction: When life looks negative, you tend to immediately drown out the problem with drugs, alcohol, or dangerous activities. This is a particularly lethal combination and often cuts life off at an early age.

Your greatest fear is that life is truly not worth living, just as you suspected all along. You need to get out of this perspective as fast as possible. Usually you need at least one professional support person on your side to do this. It's fine to anticipate difficulty, but to turn any problem into another reason for giving up and dying is not a solution.

Cynic with Greed: When life looks negative, you feel justified in your expectation that things usually go badly if allowed to and you look immediately about for something to make you feel better. You may overeat a lot or drink too much or really have a problem running up credit cards. This can create a vicious circle where your excesses make you feel bad and feeling bad drives you to more excess. This is a particularly difficult combination of traits.

Your greatest fear is that you will never be satisfied. A supportive group, such as Alcoholics Anonymous or similar associations, can be a turning point for you. You need to approach your problems more directly without trying to solve them by throwing a "goodie" in their path.

Cynic with Martyrdom: When life looks negative, you feel the walls closing in again. Problems feel like traps to you and you often feel victimized by others. The more trapped you feel the darker everything looks. You develop an unfortunate tendency to whine and nag.

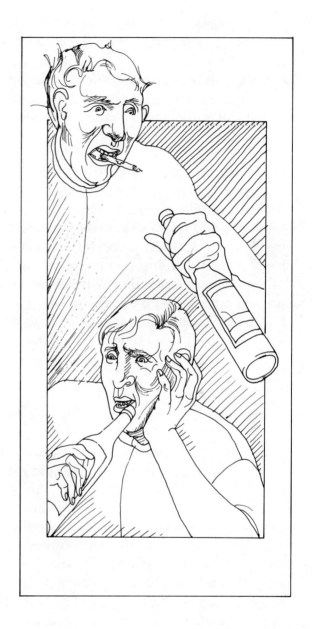

Cynic / Self-Destruction

Your greatest fear is that you will be trapped or unappreciated and it will be like that forever. You need to take more responsibility for your own actions and be more assertive in examining your options. This is extremely difficult to do without professional support. People with this set of traits often have had extremely difficult childhoods and cannot pull themselves out of Martyrdom without assistance.

Cynic with Impatience: When life looks negative, you become quite intolerant. You can get a panicky feeling that everything is going to fall apart because there is no time to come up with the appropriate solutions. You feel pushed to the limit and may be immobilized by the stress. You can feel suffocated internally as you become anxious about missed deadlines and lost opportunities.

Your biggest fear is that all is lost because there was no time to prevent catastrophe. You need to take a more realistic viewpoint. Life can be enjoyed on a day to day basis and, if you are calm and patient, you will have time to accomplish whatever is important to you. If you become more tolerant, you can have more support from loved ones.

Cynic with Stubbornness: When life looks negative you can become quite obstinate and bleak in your viewpoint. You don't want to hear anything optimistic at these times because it sounds Pollyanna-ish and foolish to you. You can dig your heels in and refuse to see a brighter picture.

Your biggest fear is that life is "going to hell in a handbasket" and this is out of your control. You need to realize that only flexibility can move you from a problem to its solution. Stubbornly standing still only makes your problem last longer. If you are willing to look at multiple options you can regain control. The quickest way to become more flexible is to be willing to look at the optimistic view of your situation as well as the negative one.

The Realist Attitude with Corresponding Obstacles

The way you view the world is to look at life as objectively as possible. You simply want to know what "is" in a situation and then you can come up with plans for dealing with it. You are usually good at seeing how things really are. You like to look at all sides of a situation but may have a difficult time making decisions. You can collect so much data that it is hard to know when to stop and actually make a choice.

Realist with Self-Deprecation: When life looks negative, you begin to lose your objectivity because of your habit of blaming yourself for whatever goes wrong in your life. You see only those facets of the situation that are negative or hurtful and forget to look at the positive factors. You are so busy beating yourself up for whatever difficulty has arisen that you lose your neutral perspective.

Your biggest fear is that the "real truth" is that "life is bad" and that you are to blame. You need to remove your focus from yourself. This will immediately present you with more opportunity to look objectively at the problem.

Realist with Arrogance: When life looks negative, you have a tendency to retreat behind a cold, somewhat superior demeanor. You become convinced that others must be to blame because you focus on their flaws and reality becomes subjective. You hate to be judged, but can become highly critical yourself when the chips are down. Nevertheless, even though you may adopt a superior looking mask, inwardly you can feel shy, embarrassed, and unable to speak out even when you know you are right.

Your greatest fear is that you will state what you believe is true and be condemned for it. You need to see that your usually realistic viewpoint can be colored with subjectivity during times of difficulty and that you may not really always be in touch with the full facts. Laying blame on yourself or others is ineffective.

Attitude: Realist

Realist with Self-Destruction: When life looks negative, you are certain that life "is" bad and a bad life does not look like a pleasant place to be. It is easy for you at these times to block out this unpleasant realization with a crutch such as drugs or alcohol. You can easily become certain that life is not worth living.

Your greatest fear is that your negative viewpoint is true. You need support from others in breaking the habit of interpreting life as worthless. You also need an inner commitment to face reality and solve your problems rather than to indulge them with negative behavior.

Realist with Greed: When life looks negative, you can convince yourself that the way out of your difficulties is to bring in some new satisfactory consumables. A new car, a hot fudge sundae, or a new lover might just solve everything.

Your greatest fear is that no matter what you do to fulfill your neediness, it won't make you feel better. You need to see that pleasurable goodies may make you feel better temporarily but are not truly solutions to the problem. The problem could crop up again because you have not really provided a solution.

Realist with Martyrdom: When life looks negative, you are totally convinced that you are a victim of circumstances. Life looks like a box that you cannot climb out of and there does not seem to be an easy solution. Anyone who might approach you with an answer will usually be met with, "Yes, but I know that won't work because . . ." Your very viewpoint negates the possibility of a solution.

Your greatest fear is that you are truly trapped in an untenable situation, possibly forever. You are convinced that no one really appreciates you. You need to become more objective and see that there are indeed viable options and solutions to your dilemma. You need to let go of your belief in your entrapment and see that there are those who truly appreciate you.

Realist with Impatience: When life looks negative, you are sure that you have to work doubly hard and fast to come to a solution in time to ward off countless difficulties. You are certain that only if you are working at your top speed can you possibly succeed. You can become cranky and intolerant of anyone who slows you down. Other people look slow and inefficient to you at these times and that can be extremely frustrating.

Your greatest fear is that everyone else is incompetent, you have to do it all by yourself, and there may not be time left to do so. You need to slow down to a steady pace and remember that there is time to handle any problem that is correctly approached. In addition you need to be more objective about your own and others skills and capabilities. What you fear is not true.

Realist with Stubbornness: When life looks negative, you feel that it is becoming difficult to control your reality. This feels very uncomfortable and can cause you to dig your heels in and refuse to move until you feel back in control of your situation. You are convinced at these moments that you are being pushed and you don't intend to stand for it. Your ideas can become quite rigid and inflexible at these times.

Your greatest fear is that you will be pushed to accept someone else's version of "what is so" and that you will not be in control of that. You need to be more flexible and objective in negative situations. There are always solutions that don't entail loss of control of your own life. You can allow others to have their opinions and their beliefs without allowing them to encroach on yours.

The Pragmatist Attitude with Corresponding Obstacles

The way you view the world is to look at what is most efficient. You often find yourself doing little things to save time and energy so as to be more productive and have your operations run more smoothly. You appreciate the practical things in life such as an efficient tool, a well laid-out office space, a smoothly-running business partnership, and so on.

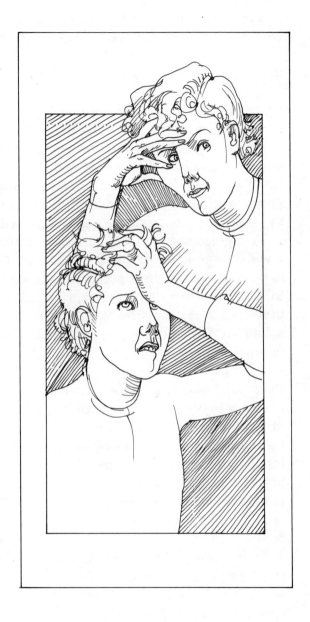

Realist / Self-Deprecation

You need to be careful not to become so efficient that you don't have any fun. For example, it saves gas to cram eight people into a six- passenger car to go to the drive-in, but it can be most uncomfortable.

Pragmatist with Self-Deprecation: When life looks negative, you can become quite uncomfortable because you feel that you must be to blame. Not only that, but you feel that you probably are responsible because of faulty planning, and you pride yourself on usually being such an efficient planner. You will run yourself down until you get around to asking yourself, "How can I salvage the pieces of this mess and put them together in some semblance of order?"

Your greatest fear is that you will waste time and energy and that it will be your fault. You need to realize that the most efficient way to proceed in difficulty is not to waste time in blaming yourself, but to proceed with an alternative plan immediately. By focusing on the problem rather than who is at fault, you can usually come to a solution almost as quickly as you would have if nothing had gone wrong.

Pragmatist with Arrogance: When life looks negative, you have a tendency to blame the nearest person including yourself for being impractical and not handling the situation correctly. You can become quite stiff and formal-looking and bring up fear and discomfort in those around you at these times. If your judgment is mainly turned toward yourself, you will immediately try to take on a perfectly competent exterior. It becomes very important to look cool and unruffled, because you can't stand anyone else's criticism at this point.

Your greatest fear is that time and energy will be wasted due to someone's stupidity or inefficiency and that you will bear the consequences of that. You need to stop wasting time blaming others or even yourself and focus on efficient solutions. Set aside what has already happened as a given and proceed freshly with the problem from that moment on. Then bring all of your efficient expertise to bear.

Pragmatist / Martyrdom

Pragmatist with Self-Destruction: When life looks negative, you proceed quite rapidly into minor or major self-destructive behavior. You don't like problems and you try to avoid them. When things look bad you may pull in habit patterns such as smoking cigarettes or even getting drugged or drunk. If you ever decide that life is absolutely not worth living or that someone else is truly expendable you could perform a practical, cold-blooded execution, if that were your choice.

Your greatest fear is that things are so chaotic and mismanaged in your life that it isn't really worth living. You need support in facing your difficulties and learning not to see them as so overwhelming. You are actually very capable and efficient at handling difficulties when you are not overwhelmed.

Pragmatist with Greed: When life looks negative, you tend to quickly arrange some minor self-indulgence to take your mind off your problem. The phrase, "When the going gets tough, the tough go shopping" was invented for you. You like to minimize your negative feelings by placating yourself with something that feels good. This often works very well in the moment, but nevertheless the problem keeps cropping up if you don't solve it.

Your greatest fear is that due to mismanagement or inefficiency on someone's part, you won't get what you want or need to be happy. You need to face your problems more directly before they get out of hand and become large and unwieldy. If you tackle a problem a piece at a time, you are quite capable of handling it and having your needs met also.

Pragmatist with Martyrdom: When life looks negative you feel that things are happening so awkwardly or inefficiently around you that you are trapped, a victim of circumstances. This can lead to quite a suffocating struggle and you may even develop an uncomfortable tendency to whine or moan about your problems at this point. Even if someone presents a practical solution to you at this time you may not be able to see how you can implement it.

Attitude: Pragmatist

Your greatest fear is that your life will fall into a chaotic mess and you will be trapped in this hopelessly inefficient tangle forever. You need to take more responsibility for seeing alternative, effective solutions and act upon these. Give up the tempting vice of complaining.

Pragmatist with Impatience: When life looks negative, you rush about trying to handle things more quickly, more efficiently and more perfectly, to stave off the impending difficulty. You can become quite frustrated or intolerant with anyone who upsets your timetable or your progress toward your goal at these times. You have to be particularly careful to be understanding of others if you are an employer or in a family setting.

Your greatest fear is that time will be wasted and that your life will end before you accomplish anything worthy of note. You need to slow down and see that you may be rushing down the path of life without smelling many of the flowers. There is joy to be found in simplicity and tranquility.

Pragmatist with Stubbornness: When life looks negative, you tend to dig your heels in and stop any activity that seems to be contributing to the problem you are having. This may halt the negative progression but does little to move you toward a practical solution. You may be quite stubborn in your refusal to listen to others' advice at this point, or consider that the advice has any practical value.

Your greatest fear is that life is spinning out of control and that you can't fix it. You need to be less dogmatic and more flexible in your search for solutions to your difficulties. Other people can be practical, too; and sometimes their ideas are even correct and workable, though different from your own.

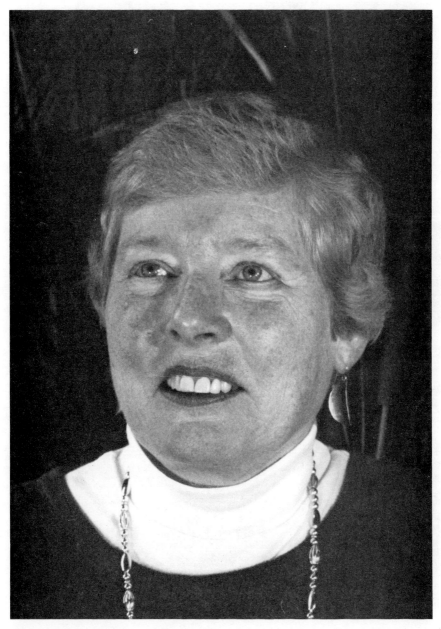

Obstacle: Self Deprecation

Obstacle: Left to Right
Self Deprecation, Stubbornness, Greed, Arrogance

Obstacle: Self Destruction

Obstacle: Martyrdom

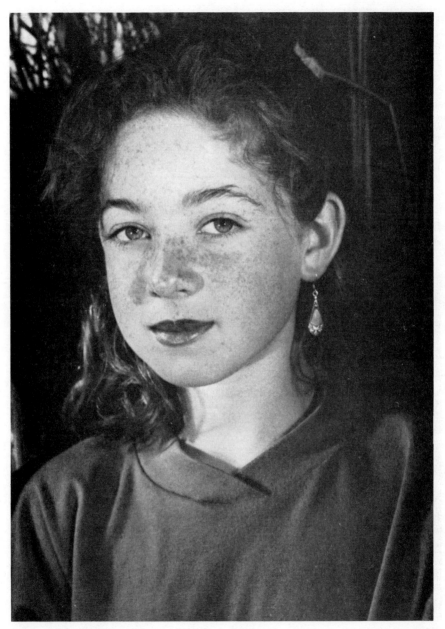

Obstacle: Greed

Obstacle: Impatience

CHAPTER FIVE

Understanding the Centers

The Centers describe *how you immediately respond* in any situation, that is, your split second reaction. Although you are capable of having every response (emotional, intellectual, and action-oriented), there is one that will characterize your response most of the time.

The three centers are described below. Find your center and read about it. For comparison read about the others. Then, you can determine in which order you tend to respond. For example: you might feel first, then think, and then act; or you might think first, then act, and feel last. This can help you to understand your response system. The center you tend to do last is the one that may need some "exercise." Optimally, you operate out of all three centers in smooth synchronization.

Intellectual Center

Your first reaction to a situation is to think about it. You experience this reaction as data pouring into and out of your head. You tend to think in words and phrases rather than pictures. You are generally quite articulate and you need to talk things out in order to understand them. Being intellectually centered does not mean that you are more intelligent than the rest of society but merely that you will use

Center: Intellectual

your mind more quickly than your body or emotions. You like to have a reason for everything and are the first person to ask, "Why?" In fact you tend to analyze everything before taking action. You value facts over your feelings or hunches and you may have difficulty understanding emotional types.

There are some drawbacks to being Intellectually Centered. There is a time lag before your emotions and your ability to take action catch up to your thoughts. This means that you might think something is a good idea, but then realize the next day that negative feelings about it have slowly surfaced. Likewise, you might not act on a good idea for quite some time while you continue to analyze it.

The contemporary United States culture encourages people to be more intellectually centered.

Emotional Center

Your first reaction to a situation is a strong emotional or perceptive "hit" about what is going on. You cannot always explain or articulate your feelings, you just "know" what you feel is true. Your perceptions are often highly accurate even though they are not based on logic or data collecting. You tend to think in pictures or whole scenarios. Your accurate emotional perceptions are the bane of your intellectually centered friends who need to know the reason why something is true. You can become adept at satisfying their needs by pulling in logical, back-up data for what you already know. However; the truth is, you just pull in data to satisfy them and make your knowledge look more legitimate.

You feel an immediate, terrible impact when something unbalancing, upsetting, or tragic occurs. You can be so emotionally overwhelmed at these times that you feel frozen and unable to do anything about the immediate situation.

Traditionally, emotionally centered people have been valued for their ability to express through decorating, drama, art, singing, and music.

Center: Emotional

Latin cultures tend to promote feelings and to believe in emotionally centered people. They hold honest perceptivity as being more useful than intellectualizations.

Moving Center

Your first reaction to a situation is to act upon it. You are very physical and you like to handle situations in a "hands on" fashion. You want to "do something" when you have a problem. You are survival-oriented and well in touch with your body's needs and wants. You have many handy physical skills. You are probably good at sports, dance, and skills that require coordination.

Your body tends to be in constant motion even when you are sitting still. You change positions and locations in the room often and this extends to changing your neighborhood, job, and other activities more often than others. You will tend to travel more as well.

You tend to act first and think later. The drawbacks to this are obvious. There is also an emotional time lag, so you may become enrolled in a project and then realize that you are not enjoying it.

Obsessive behavior can develop in extreme cases where an action brings up a feeling that causes you to repeat the action again and again — for example, playing slot machines or video games over and over to experience each quick emotional thrill. Addictions follow this same pattern.

Traditionally, moving centered people are welcome and common in survival settings like the jungle, desert or arctic. You are considered the best hunters, craftsman, builders, and soldiers.

Center: Moving

CHAPTER SIX

What It Means to Have a Role

Your role reflects who you are, in your most intimate values, abilities, and beingness. It can be somewhat obscured by cultural values as well as parental and social conditioning. Because of this you may appear to be just like your parents. But when you look through this layer of conditioning, your true nature emerges and your role becomes more apparent.

For this reason, your role becomes most noticeable after substantial life experience, usually by the mid-thirties.

Servers and Priests are the Inspirational Roles; Artisans and Sages, the Expressive Roles; Warriors and Kings, the Action Roles; and Scholar, the Assimilative Role.

The Server Role

As a **Server** you get deep satisfaction from nurturing others. You are usually a friendly, approachable, modest person. People love you and are inspired by you because you are willing to think of their needs as well as your own.

You are very good at controlling from behind the scenes. For example, you can make a large dinner party look effortless. You specialize in close, one-on-one contact with others. You never lose touch with the needs of an individual loved one while you are trying

Role: Server

Role: Server

Role: Server

to handle the needs of the crowd. You are excellent at personal touches like serving hot cocoa on cold days or taking an hour out of your busy weekend to fix a friend's car.

On the other hand, you may neglect your own needs and become overcommitted to others' programs. You may have a tendency to become intrusive or smothering in your attempts to assist your loved ones.

Remember to take good care of yourself or you'll be too frazzled to do anyone else much good. Also keep in mind that you deserve respect and high self-esteem for being such an inspirational and unselfish person.

We have observed that countries such as China and India apparently have a great number of Servers in their population. We conjecture that at one time there were a great many more Servers in the United States. Recently with the move to a more creative, productive, and self-oriented society, the numbers have dwindled down to about 10% of the population.* This apparent decrease in Servers has been paralleled by a corresponding increase in the divorce rate and the general dissolution of the family unit.

Servers then, are the glue that hold the fabric of society together.

Servers are: Nurturers, helpmates, healers, caretakers.

The Priest Role

As a **Priest** you have a special talent for being able to recognize where people are most blocked in their development. You are usually an inspiring, motivating, dedicated person with a magnetic personality. You are very compassionate toward mankind in general and you hate to see someone lose their path. You are good at discussing personal difficulties with people gently but forcefully and are willing to nudge them toward a more enlightened experience. Most of

*Our figures on percentages of individuals of a certain Role come from results compiled by testing volunteers across the U.S. with the Essence and Personality Profile.

Role: Priest

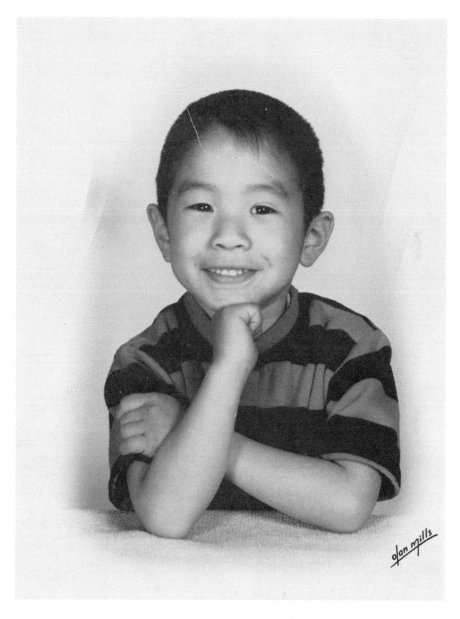

Role: Priest

Role: Priest

you have a liking for large congregations of souls who look to you for some spiritual guidance. Even those of you that are more shy and quiet like to think of doing something for mankind as a whole. All of you would like to make a positive difference in the world during your lifetime.

Be careful not to run roughshod over others as you attempt to improve them or the world — even if you do have their best interests at heart. Friends don't always take kindly to having their lives rearranged.

We have observed the role of Priest is so specialized that there are not many of them in the population at large: only about 3% to 5%. The world needs fewer shepherds than members of the flock.

Recently, as many traditional and orthodox religions have begun to dwindle in numbers, the need for leadership by individual Priests has increased. Therefore, your presence is felt more in everyday life.

Priests are: Preachers, consciences, goads.

The Artisan Role

As an **Artisan**, you are very aware of and affected by your environment. You tend to subtly create the mood wherever you are. For example, if you are happy, a party shines; if you are sad, it can be subdued, even if you are a wallflower and don't think that you are participating. You are a creative, innovative, visionary person who is usually one step ahead of the crowd. You have an unusual artistic, eccentric flair, and a style all your own. Whether you use it or not, you usually have a fair amount of artistic talent and interest in the arts.

On the other hand, you may be a daydreamer living in a world of your own creation, deceiving yourself about reality. You may find it difficult to make it in the material world. You can get so out of touch with objective reality that some of you forget who you really are.

Try to remember that the simple truths in life are not complex.

Role: Artisan

Role: Artisan

Role: Artisan

When you take things down to a minimum you can feel more secure, and less like the universe is one chaotic mess. You need to build bridges between your far-reaching visions and the mainstream realities of others or you can feel quite cut off.

We have observed that since the 1960's there has been more demand in United States society that people be in touch with their inner creativity. We believe that this is accountable for the quiet subtle rise in the Artisan population; presently about 20%.

Artisans are: Artists, innovators, trendsetters, inventors, eccentrics.

The Sage Role

As a **Sage** your job is to find out everything important there is to know and spread that knowledge to as many others as possible, through humor and entertainment. You are a light-hearted, wise, articulate individual. You hate to grow up or lose your childlike wonder towards the world. You excel verbally and make a great lecturer, communicator, or comedian. Most of you love being the center of attention and are the life of the party.

On the other hand, you can be loud, tasteless, or childish if you aren't careful. You also have a tendency to be overly garrulous and talk the ears off your listeners.

You need to avoid scandalous gossip which you tend to love. Juicy stories always grab your attention but when you spread them you can become slanderous. It would be easier on your listeners if you give them just a kernel of basic information, at times.

We have observed that Sages have wound their way into the entertainment and media fields in large numbers, particularly since the advent of film, television, and radio. Even though these Sages are very visible, we have found that the percentage of Sages in the population as a whole is quite small, probably not more than 15%.

Sages are: Communicators, entertainers, teachers and tricksters.

Role: Sages

Role: Sage

Role: Sage

The Warrior Role

As a **Warrior** you are in charge of defending and protecting society. You are a productive, organized, persuasive individual always out to protect the underdog. You have an excellent head for business and are usually viewed by others as competent and powerful. You are the most focused of individuals, are good strategists, and you "get the job done". Under your tough exterior you are actually a tender-hearted individual. You tend to be patriotic to a cause or country and are monetarily conservative.

On the other hand, you can be overly coercive and argumentative. You are a pushover for a hard luck story and occasionally too naive for your own good. You are subject to tunnel vision in pursuit of your principles.

You need to remember to look at the bigger picture and widen your focus. You can look scary and intimidating to those around you, so be gentle with them. Remember, be persuasive rather than coercive.

We have observed that the U.S.A. is rapidly becoming a predominantly Warrior culture. The presence of Warriors in the population has moved up to approximately 30% in recent years. With this kind of influence, even non-Warriors will be drawn in to the productive, ambitious type of energy that Warriors represent.

Warriors are: Strategists, advocates, organizers, Business-people, Rocks-of-Gibralter.

Role: Warrior

Role: Warrior

Role: Warrior

The King Role

As a **King** you are a born leader. You may have a regal bearing and inspire great loyalty from others. You are never satisfied until you feel you have mastered whatever you are attempting to accomplish. You have a good grasp of the big picture and are excellent at orchestrating large complex projects. You are a natural delegator: you can see which person is best suited for each job and charismatic enough to get them all to work together. You can be quite magnanimous and generous with your loyal followers when you are feeling good. You usually feel responsible for their well being and will take great efforts to provide for them. In fact you are willing to take the ultimate responsibility.

On the other hand, at your worst you can be tyrannical and overbearing. You have a strong tendency towards perfectionism and tend to apply your exacting standards to others. Remember that if you ease up on yourself and those who serve you, you will be able to lead more effectively. You do not want to inspire a mutiny.

We have observed that there are very few Kings in the population, 1-2%, and often you are found in positions of power or authority.

Kings are: Adepts, masters, leaders, orchestrators.

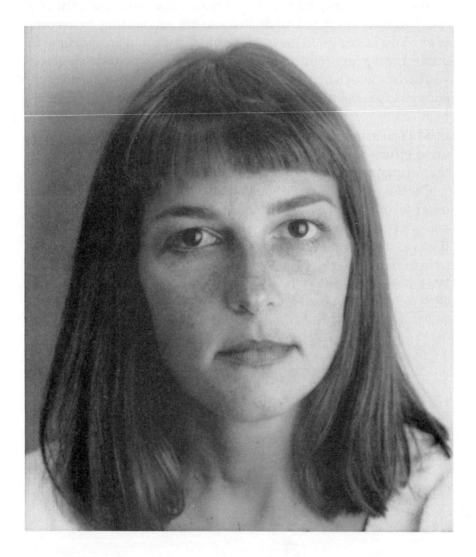

Role: King

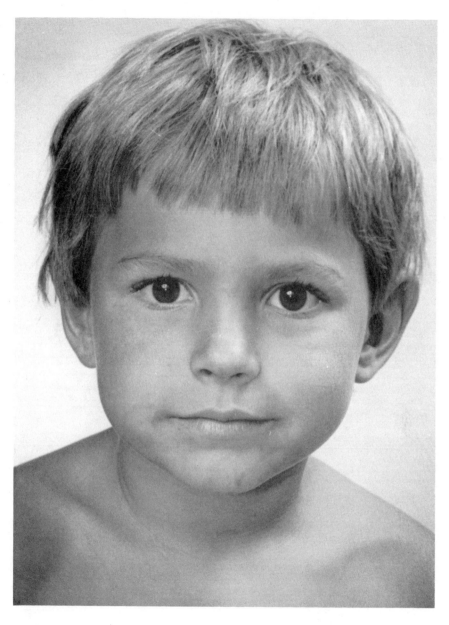

Role: King

Role: King

The Scholar Role

As a **Scholar,** you are a natural observer, arbitrator, and a born philosopher. You like to maintain a neutral perspective and you are very good at seeing all sides of an issue. You are a natural student with a high level of curiosity and a great willingness to risk in order to satisfy your thirst for new knowledge. You love to experiment with things to find out what would happen "if..." This makes you a good scientist if you wish to actualize this aspect of yourself. Often you have a love of books and like to take copious notes in order to learn something new. You are the most eclectic of all the roles, often having more than one profession as well as numerous hobbies. In addition you are visionary, adventurous, and you usually have good judgement.

On the other hand, you can blend in too much with the wallpaper in your effort to maintain neutrality. You are often so busy assimilating what is going on around you that you don't share your vast experience and may even be considered dull company. The phrase "absent-minded professor" was coined for you.

Watch out for your tendency to over-intellectualize. Theorizing isn't the same as being knowledgeable. You'd have a lot more fun and be more involved if you participate more noticeably.

We have observed that Scholars, although sprinkled throughout the population, tend to cluster in academic settings such as universities, scientific projects, and libraries. Nevertheless you may be found in almost any line of work.

Scholars are: Students, philosophers, adventurers, anthropologists.

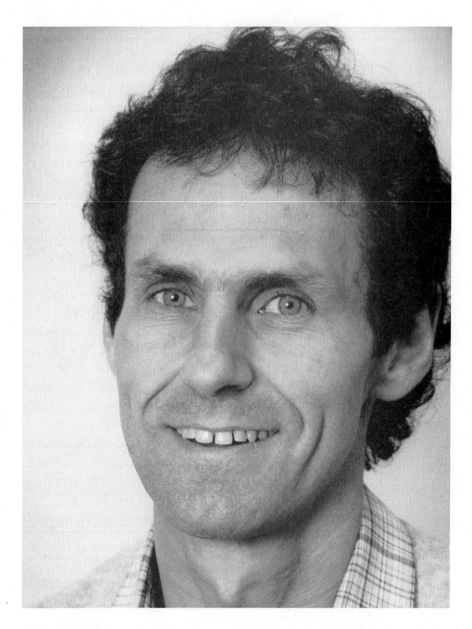

Role: Scholar

Role: Scholar

Role: Scholar

CHAPTER SEVEN

Famous Examples

Now that you have discovered your key traits, and have read an explanation of how they work, you are probably wondering how all six of these pieces fall together to form a personality. The best way to give you a feel for how these six traits blend together is to describe how they show up in particular individuals.

Here we describe seven famous people, each with a different role and combination of traits. We'll show you how their particular combination of traits mainfested in the way they led their lives.

These seven famous people each exhibit a particular way that the traits might show up in a person's life. The way another person uses those traits might be very different from these exceptional people. However they are good examples of using one's traits to the fullest of one's potential.

Florence Nightingale: Server

Florence Nightingale: 1820-1910

Role: Server
Goal: Submission
Mode: Observation
Attitude: Spiritualist
Obstacle: Impatience
Center: Intellectual Center

Florence Nightingale was the founder of the present day nursing profession. She revolutionized nursing care to make it an honorable, clean, and dignified profession. She overrode her wealthy family's opposition to study nursing at a German institute at a time when hospitals were dirty and disreputable. At thirty three she became superintendant at a hospital in London and the next year the Secretary of War of Great Britain asked her to take charge of nursing the wounded soldiers in the Crimean War. In two years of tireless effort she saved countless lives and brought world reforms in hospital administration and nursing work. She became a world authority on scientific care of the sick and the United States used her advice for setting up military hospitals during the Civil War. The strain of overwork and illness she suffered in the Crimean forced her to become a semi-invalid but for the next fifty years, ministers, authors, reformers, and politicians sought her for her expert advice on health care. Her correspondence affected health conditions all over the world. She was the first woman to receive the British Order of Merit.

We feel that Florence is an excellent example of a Server due to her dedication to nurturing her fellow man. Florence was born to wealthy British parents while they were living abroad in Florence, Italy. Early on she demonstrated talent in the management of her family's large household. These management skills stood her in good stead later on in her career as hospital administrator. Servers are known for their ability to control and manage quietly and smoothly.

Florence enjoyed caring for visiting children and sick farmers on her father's estate. At age sixteen she decided to never marry but to dedicate herself to the service of others. She declined the many parties of her social class in the Victorian Age and spent her time studying health and considering reforms for the poor. A true mark of the server is to avoid the public eye, and Florence, true to fashion, always shunned publicity. Her unflagging dedication to the wounded during the Crimean War is further evidence of her Server temperament.

We believe that Florence demonstrates the key combination of Submission as a Goal with Observation as a Mode. People with a Goal of Submission are always happiest once they devote themselves to a cause. They want to submit to that cause and their own needs become second. This is certainly the case with Florence. She never married or enjoyed her wealthy station in life as did the other young women of her day but instead was tirelessly dedicated to the cause of reforming the nursing profession.

A person in Observation Mode clearly sees what needs to be done in a given situation and Florence was an expert at this. With thirty eight nurses she walked into a huge, dirty, Turkish barracks with five hundred bleeding, injured and neglected British soldiers. Within days she had organized it into a clean efficient hospital with herself patrolling the lengthy corridors at night to check on the injured. Another mark of her Observation Mode was her awareness and understanding of the suffering and illness that was outside her social class.

As far as Attitude and Obstacle go, we feel that Florence was a Spiritualist in Impatience. Spiritualists are always capable of viewing the utopian possibilities in any situation. It would probably take a Spiritualist to contemplate as large a task as changing the nursing profession world-wide. This looks like it goes beyond Idealism which tends to take a situation and patch it to make it better. (An Idealist looks at step A and envisions step B. A Spiritualist looks at step A and envisions step Z.) Impatience seems to be the motivating force that led her to study nursing in the face of her family's opposition since impatience always makes a person headstrong. It also shows up in her countless letters demanding supplies from British military officials until she drove them to distraction; and, in fact, initially alienated them. Impatient people continually strive for perfection and often sleep little. Both of these are known to be traits that showed up in Florence's personality.

We believe her to be Intellectually Centered because of the amount of book study she put herself through with little family or class encouragement. One of her most important programs in the Crimean military hospitals, once she had them running well, was to teach convalescing soldiers reading and writing. Intellectually centered people tend to be horrified by illiteracy.

Saint Joan of Arc: Priest

Saint Joan of Arc: 1412-1431

Role: Priest
Goal: Submission
Mode: Aggression
Attitude: Spiritualist
Obstacle: Martyrdom
Center: Emotional

Joan of Arc was a French peasant girl who led the French Army to victory over the English under the reign of Charles VII. She claimed to have visions given to her by God that would enable her to personally lead the French troops to victory through divine guidance and perfect military strategy. She was renowned for her personal bravery and won over the support of the French commanders through her skill and prowess as a military leader. Eventually she was captured by the Bergundians, who sold her to their allies, the English, whereupon she was burned at the stake as a witch. She died at age nineteen and was declared a Saint in the Roman Catholic Church in 1920.

We feel that Joan of Arc is an excellent example of the Role of Priest. Her relationship with God was of paramount importance to her and she felt driven to devote herself to what she saw as God's Will, even if it cost her her life. Priests also have a tendency to be incredibly inspirational and capable of gaining the support and following of even highly skeptical people. The ability of a seventeen year old girl to impress the king of France and all the seasoned soldiers of his army enough to convince them to give her command over all of the king's troops, is a truly Priestly feat.

We feel that Joan had the key combination of Submission as a Goal and Aggression as a Mode, an unusual configuration. Her Submission Goal shows up clearly in her total dedication to a cause, above and beyond herself. She gave up every facet of her young life to ensure the installation of Charles VII on his rightful throne. She then would have willingly retired but on his orders she continued to fight until her eventual capture and death, an act of total dedication. People with a Goal of Submission can be notoriously neglectful of their own personal lives when they submit to a fervent cause.

Aggression as a Mode is highly dynamic and charismatic as well as aggressive and energetic. We feel that Joan is a perfect example of a person charismatic enough to impress kings and soldiers and aggressive enough to fight fearlessly in numerous battles. She was injured on a number of occasions and always managed to rally to the next engagement with the English. It would take an incredibly charismatic person to wind up in her military position being an illiterate young peasant girl of the thirteenth century.

The combination of the two was immensely powerful because the cause to which she submitted was so empowered by her aggressive ability.

In Attitude and Obstacle, we believe that Joan was a Spiritualist in Martyrdom. Spiritualists are always ready to believe that their visions can be made into reality no matter how far fetched, and Joan was definitely a visionary of this type. Joan had an incredible capacity to see what "could be", considering her humble beginnings and lack of formal training in the military arts.

A Spiritualist in Martyrdom would always be expected to martyr herself for her vision and we feel that Joan did exactly that. Key elements of Martyrdom are complete selflessness and a sense of being trapped in a destiny not of their own making. We can see this especially in her agreement to continue fighting for the king even after she had completed her goal of seeing him crowned. She continued to fight even after she had been seriously injured and felt no personal desire to continue.

We feel that Joan of Arc was very likely Emotionally Centered, driven by her feelings and her sense of what would be the right thing to do rather than any intellectual knowledge. She was completely uneducated and could neither read nor write but operated from her inner feelings and guidance in her battles.

The combination of Emotional Centering with her Priestly role, Goal of Submission, Aggression Mode, and Spiritualist Attitude made Joan a uniquely effective and powerful force in the world.

George Washington Carver: Artisan

George Washington Carver: 1864-1943

Role: Artisan

Goal: Growth
Mode: Perseverance

Attitude: Pragmatist
Obstacle: Martyrdom

Center: Intellectual

George Washington Carver, an American Black man, was born a slave in Missouri in 1864. As he grew older, the study of plants and rocks fascinated him and after he was freed from slavery, he became known as The Plant Doctor. He worked his way through Iowa State College, became a botanist, and eventually revolutionized the agriculture of the South. He developed more than three hundred products from the peanut alone. He was not only a brilliant inventor, and botanist, but also such a fine artist that he became a Fellow in the Royal Society of Arts in London, an honor given to few Americans of his day.

Artisans typically shine in the arts or they become highly creative and inventive in other fields. Washington Carver was so prolific that he managed to do both. In typical Artisan fashion he was oriented toward discovering and doing things that no one had ever done before. Like many Artisans he was a painter in his spare time and liked to work in other art forms as well. He seems to have been influenced by a Scholar in childhood, who encouraged his curious side.

We believe that he shows the key combinations of Growth as a goal with Perseverance Mode. People in Growth are constantly evolving trying to find new paths in life. They forge ahead tirelessly motivated by the desire to expand themselves and develop their skills and talents. Certainly, Carver demonstrates this trait as exhibited by his desire to not only develop himself but to contribute to the evolution of mankind as well.

His Perseverance shows up clearly in his dogged pursuit of higher education despite his background of slavery and poverty, at a time when the obstacles to Blacks were almost insurmountable. It would also take great perseverance and disipline to relentlessly experiment enough to come up with the hundreds of new products he discovered in his lifetime. When we put the two together, Growth and Perseverance, we see in Carver a person who would not be deterred in his push for evolution on many fronts.

When we look at Carver's Attitude and Obstacle combination we see that he exhibits the traits of Pragmatism (Attitude) and Martyrdom (Obstacle). It takes groundedness and practicality to be successfully involved in scientific study to the degree that Carver was. It takes a practical mind as well to be able to overcome the enormous obstacles of birth into slavery and poverty, being a racial minority, and struggling through the scientific field of endeavor while facing racial discrimination.

The Martyrdom exhibits itself in Carver's personal notes and his self sacrifice to the scientific field. He does not readily and apparently show any of the more negative qualities that go along with the Obstacle of Martyrdom. His success in life demonstrates his ability to overcome the obstacle of feeling victimized, by whites and blacks of his day alike.

Carver's Centering was clearly Intellectual. He was able to proceed logically through the many steps in the scientific process, to invent new products and discover new uses for known plants, nuts, and fruits. In addition he was a college professor at Iowa State College, and Tuskegee Institute, positions requiring the ability to speak articulately about science to others.

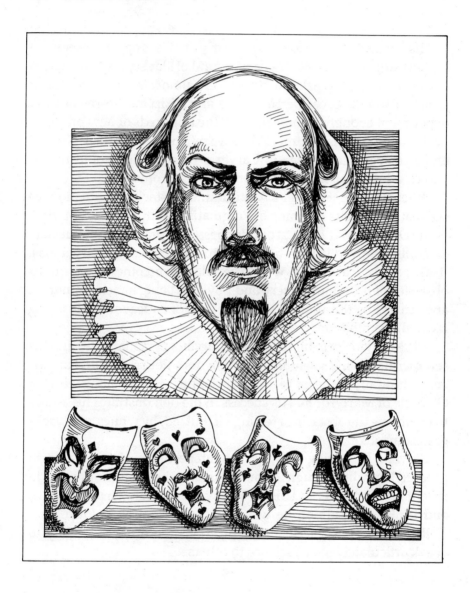

William Shakespeare: Sage

William Shakespeare: 1564-1616

Role: Sage
Goal: Growth
Mode: Observation
Attitude: Pragmatist
Obstacle: Arrogance
Center: Intellectual or Emotional

William Shakespeare remains the most powerful and revered dramatist and playwright that the world has known, and is considered by many to be most famous poet in the English language.   Born in England in 1564, by the age of twenty eight he was already a well known actor and playwright. During his lifetime, he was the author of thirty eight plays, numerous poems, and non-dramatic works. He exemplified an Elizabethan style in attitude toward poetry, music, and the politics of the day. He died at age fifty-two, a wealthy and respected member of society whose personal artistic patron was King James the First.

We feel that Shakespeare is an excellent example of a Sage because Sages are renowned for their communication skills and their mastery of their native language as well as other languages. They shine in the fields of comedy, tradgedy, drama, and any media event performed for the public. Shakespeare's works, highly public, took the world by storm and influenced not only the people of his day but also all of us who still use the English language. He is famous for inventing innumerable words and phrases still in use today. This reflects Sages' creative manipulation of words and their ability to disseminate in such a way that their message is completely comprehensible to persons of any social strata of society.

We believe that his Goal and Mode key combination would be that of Growth and Observation. His plays and other works show evolution of the characters and generally teach a lesson to the characters themselves and to the audience. This is very much a quality that would show up in the works of somebody with the goal of Growth. In addition we see that his life was extremely active involving non-stop projects, ambitions, and new endeavors in widely ranging fields. This is another sign of a life Goal of Growth.

It is highly likely that his Mode was Observation because one of Shakespeare's main characteristics was his amazing knowledge of such a wide variety of subjects as diverse as music, law, seamanship, military science, politics, history, psychology, art, and sports. His knowledge was so accurate about so many things that lawyers have tried to prove that he was a lawyer and sailors have tried to prove that he had seagoing experience, even though none of that appears to be true. Shakespeare was known for his amazing ability to reproduce verbatim conversations that he had overheard. This takes powerful observation skills.

We feel that Shakespeare demonstrated the key combination of Pragmatist Attitude and Arrogance as Obstacle. He was able to view the world from such a multiplicity of perspectives that we feel it would have been beyond the natural optimism of the Idealist or natural pessimism of the Cynic to have such a wide repertoire of perspectives. Pragmatists can take on the point of view of any other attitude if it sounds practical to do so, and Shakespeare had that facility. He also was shown historically to be an excellent and sensible businessman, investing in solid real estate and stock in theatres and theatrical companies of this day. He was a practical and successful businessman.

From everything known about him, Shakespeare thought well of himself and respected his own work highly. In his plays, he took pleasure in lampooning others who seemed to be overly puffed up about their own importance. It is typical for a person to make fun of qualities that they see somewhat in themselves. In this case, that quality was Arrogance.

When Shakespeare was severly criticized he went out of his way to appear civilized and collected to his detractor's friends. He did not like to show any vulnerabilty to criticism but could in fact be quite critical of others. This is a pragmatic, arrogant style.

We feel that a case could be made as far as centering goes, for Shakespeare to be either Emotionally or Intellectually Centered. He had great empathy for people from all walks of life and seemed to easily imagine what it would be like to be a merchant's daughter, a pauper, a blind man, or a king for example. That amount of keen insight is often found in those that are Emotionally Centered. However he is also known as one of the greatest intellectual geniuses of all time and his incredible literary ability and language skills are generally those that would be found in an Intellectually Centered person. Since all people use all centers, it may have been that his Emotional Center was as developed as his Intellectual Center or vice-versa. This is a sign of a healthy and balanced person.

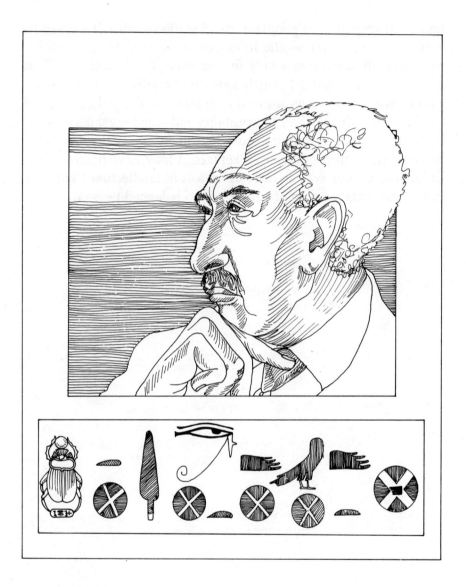

Anwar El-Sadat: Warrior

Anwar El-Sadat: 1818-1981

Role: Warrior
Goal: Acceptance
Mode: Observation
Attitude: Stoic
Obstacle: Arrogance
Center: Intellectual

Anwar El-Sadat was an Egyptian army officer and politician who was president of Egypt from 1970 until his assasination in 1981. He was also one of the key people who orchestrated the Egyptian revolution from British control and helped to secure Egypt's indepedence in 1952. He was famous for expelling the Soviets from Egypt in order to increase Egypt's independence and he won the Nobel Peace Prize in 1978 for engineering the peace agreement between Egypt and Israel.

We believe Anwar El-Sadat is a good example of the Warrior Role. He devoted himself to the military, after stating that he could see no other career for himself, and worked tirelessly for the political cause of freedom for his country. Warriors tend to be patriotic, nationalistic, and operate from their principles even more so than people of other roles. Another great skill of Warriors is their ability to organize and Anwar, when he was only twenty-one, organized almost singlehandedly the Free Officers Association that eventually overthrew the British rule.

Another key Warrior trait exhibited by Anwar is the ability to persuade and, if necessary, coerce to get the job done. Anwar was able to persuade fellow army officers to turn away from British rule and form an independent Egypt. He used coercion in expelling all the Soviets from his country and securing independence shortly after he became president. He used coercion as well to force more equitable distribution of agricultural lands within Egypt, infuriating the rich and pleasing the poor.

We feel that Anwar exhibits the key combination of Acceptance (Goal) and Observation (Mode) Although he lived in turbulent times for his country, he always spoke of the importance of love and his paramount objective was to make his people happy. One of the most significant places where this combination shows up is in his writing about experiences in solitary confinement while imprisoned by the British in the 1940's under horrific conditions. Though denied even a bed and clean food he regarded his last months in prison as the "happiest period of my life," because of the observations he made about his true nature during that time. He felt that he gained peace of mind, self-love, incredible endurance and a closeness to God throughout his ordeal. He accepted that this was a necessary and helpful period for him to have gone through and he felt that his self-knowledge increased tremendously. These facts demonstrate the clear functions of the Acceptance-Observation combination.

His desire to observe clearly before taking any action was obvious in his work under President Nasser wherein he mainly observed what was happening politically and wrote about it in his newspaper, rather than taking part in the power struggles.

It would seem that Anwar had a combination of Stoic Attitude and Arrogance as an Obstacle. Stoics are very hard to read and their attitude is almost indecipherable and Anwar used this quality again and again to his political advantage. No one knew what he was thinking. Even the intelligence agencies of five different countries did not know what he was planning before the overthrow of King Farouk and the British government.

We see Arrogance in his continual and dedicated belief in himself as the mover and shaker of modern Egyptian history. He obviously felt that he, more than anyone else, was capable of leading his country through the difficult period of early independence and he felt quite secure in his ability to do the job well. We believe that this was fairly mild Arrogance because, in his eleven years of rulership he did a very good job in the eyes of his people. The combination of

Stoic and Arrogance would have made him appear as an exceptionally formidable man masking the flexibility and innate kindness of a person in Acceptance.

Anwar El-Sadat was probably Intellectually Centered. He read avidly, pursued knowledge fervently, and philosophized intellectually about life continually. He was a highly articulate person who used strategy and logic to persuade people to his ends. This is the mark of an intellectually centered Warrior.

Alexander the Great: King

Alexander the Great 356-323 B.C.

Role: King
Goal: Dominance
Mode: Power
Attitude: Idealist
Obstacle: Greed
Center: Moving

Alexander the Great was King of Macedonia as well as one of the greatest generals in history. He spent his life amassing an enormous empire through his brilliant military strategy, strength, and leadership skills.

We chose Alexander the Great as an exemplar because of his qualities as the quintessential king. In his youth, in typical King fashion, he mastered all the physical, intellectual, and diplomatic skills necessary to become a great leader later in his life. He became a strong, fearless fighter, famous for taming a wild stallion when only fourteen years old. He studied Greek literature, philosophy, anthropology, biology, and zoology under Aristotle to make him the most educated soldier of his day. He also mastered diplomatic skills by working with ambassadors to his father's kingdom from many foreign cultures. He became an ambassador to Athens when he was only eighteen years old.

From the time he was twenty, when he became the King of Macedonia, until his death at the age of thirty three, he conquered most of what at that time was the civilized world. His King qualities show up as well in the organizational and administrative abilities of such a large empire. He organized so well; that four hundred years later, Christianity was able to spread rapidly and easily through the entire region due to the still cohesive trade routes that he left behind.

We feel that Alexander demonstrates the key combination of Dominance and Power as his Goal and Mode. As you will recall a goal of Dominance is always geared toward control, winning, and competitions. With Power as an adjunct Mode, the dominant person will take control with full force and authority. When Alexander was still a lad he was quoted as saying, "My father will get ahead of me in everything and leave nothing great for me to do". These are typical words one might hear from a Power and Dominance person in a moment of insecurity. He was afraid that he might be blocked from his great ambition and motivation.

As far as Attitude and Obstacle goes, Alexander looks to us to be an Idealist in Greed. Idealists are always anticipating the next experience. They are rarely satisfied with the status quo and are constantly searching for how a situation can be improved. When combined with Greed, there is an underlying fear that some bottomless pit will never be filled and a person develops a crutch to alter his mood. Alexander's habit of being in a state of continual conquest seems to us to be a good illustration of the Idealist-Greed combination. His mastery skills and his dominance and power thrust enabled him to pleasantly fulfill his greed on such a grand scale.

As far as centering goes, we feel that Alexander's Moving Center wins out over his Emotional and Intellectual abilities, although these were great as well. To be such a skillful soldier, general, and have such highly co-ordinated physical skills would entail having a very strong Moving centeredness. Moving Centered people love to be constantly on the move and Alexander was never happy sitting still for very long. He was continually moving his armies from one place to another even to the point of mutiny at one time, only stopping to consolidate his position as long as was necessary. As you can see, a person with this combination of traits is a force with which to contend. A King with with these traits could hardly fail in what he set out to do. Of course, not all persons with this combination would set out to do the same thing. In modern times Alexander might look more like an international, corporate mogul; swallowing up corporations as he traveled.

Galileo Galilei: Scholar

Galileo Galilei

Role: Scholar

Goal: Growth
Mode: Observation

Attitude: Realist
Obstacle: Stubbornness

Center: Intellectual

Galileo Galilei, an Italian physicist and mathematician, was the founder of the modern scientific method. He discovered the law of the pendulum and the "law of falling bodies". He also invented new tools to be used in mathematics, physics, and drafting. He improved the telescope to such a degree that he could study the heavens in detail and this led to important new discoveries in astronomy.

He was one of the first people to ignore superstition and go straight for scientific fact. Because of this, his theories and observations were controversial, especially since many of them were in contradiction to the teachings of Aristotle, who was the accepted authority of the day. He irritated the Roman Catholic Church to such a degree that they forced him to appear before the inquisition and as a result he was confined by the church to his villa for the last ten years of his life. Nevertheless, during that time he wrote extensively on all of his discoveries. His works went on to profoundly effect the scientific community many years after his death.

We feel that Galileo is a good example of a Scholar. Scholars not only love intellectualizing and studying new things but they also have a tendency to put their fingers in many pies at once. In addition to Galileo's work in astronomy, mathematics, and physics, he was a fine musician, had a reputation as an excellent painter, was a good craftsman, and a student of medicine and philosophy. He also shows a Scholar's bent in his pursuit of knowledge and truth even in the face of the opposition of his day. It is a classic Scholarly trait to look at what is actually so, without allowing fears or other emotional states to interfere with logical process. Galileo demonstrated this quality of neutrality and objectivity.

We believe that Galileo demonstrated the key combinations of Growth (Goal) and Observation (Mode). People in Growth are continually evolving and creating new problems and challenges for themselves and the world. Their lives are about seeking out the unknown and exploring new potentials. Galileo's career as an inventor and seeker of new possibilities showed a strong growth trait. People with a Goal of Growth are often forward thinkers and sometimes irritate those around them that are stolidly conservative, obviously a phenomenon in Galileo's life.

Galileo is almost a perfect example of how one could use Observation so completely and thoroughly. It would take quite an observer to discover a basic law of physics like the pendulum theory simply by watching a swinging lamp in the cathedral as Galileo did at the tender age of twenty. His many discoveries were directly related to his powers of observation. Indeed his work with the telescope is proof enough of his penchant for growing through observing.

Galileo is a good example of someone with the key combinations of Realist (Attitude) and Stubbornness (Obstacle). Realists are rarely if ever sidetracked by superstitious flights of fantasy, or opinions based on emotions. Galileo was the inventor of the modern scientific method, an approach that bases its findings on logical and provable scientific experimentation. This is the type of approach that would have been founded by a realist. Though little is known about Galileo's personal life, the very fact that he defied the Catholic Inquisition, even temporarily, to stand up for his theories, shows an indication of Stubbornness.

Flexible people probably did not attempt to face down the Inquisition. It had too much power and could torture a person to death on a whim. Galileo would have had to rally tremendous support from his followers and have a firm stance of conviction toward his own beliefs to survive this encounter, yet he did.

It seems obvious that Galileo was also Intellectually Centered. He was not only highly educated but based all of his life's work on intellectual processes and was clearly a scientific genius. He demonstrated a continual thirst and pursuit of knowledge which is an Intellectual trait. Galileo was both a Scholar and Intellectually Centered, making him doubly oriented toward the pursuit of higher truth.

AFTERWORD

Not everyone with the same combination of traits will have the same impact on the world nor necessarily manifest these traits the same way. Should you have the same traits as Shakespeare, for example, you will not necessarily be a literary genius. You will find your own expression of these traits based on your culture, family, background and personal choices.

Nevertheless, in basic ways some of your patterns will be predictable. When your behavior is predictable, it is also possible to plan for it and shift it in positive ways. You can learn to anticipate negative scenarios based on your habitual patterns and take the necessary steps to promote well being instead.   If you have a Pragmatist Attitude with an Obstacle of Arrogance under stress, you can predict that you will get dogmatic and overbearing. If you can see this coming you are in a much better position to steer clear of this pattern.

When you understand the traits of the people around you, you are in a much better position to communicate with them and work with them more constructively.   If you know someone has a Goal of Growth with a Mode of Passion, you would be foolish to give them a repetitive, unchanging work load. By the same token, if you know someone has a Goal of Dominance and is in the Power Mode, its a good bet they can handle leadership and responsibility. When you consider roles, a Warrior can be very good at organization, while you might like to pull in a Sage for communication, fun, and entertainment.

The more you understand the key traits and combinations the better you will become at identifying them in other people. At first you can have people take the Essence and Personality Profile Questionnaire to help you identify their traits if they are willing and interested. However, before long, with practice you will be able to notice some traits simply by being with people. This will make you more proficient at human understanding and hopefully a more accepting, tolerant person yourself.

Always remember that no matter what a person's traits are, their use of them is unique. Just as you think you have them pegged, they will do something unexpected. This keeps people exciting and interesting and not too compartmentalized. Still, with a good knowledge of your own key traits and those of the people in your life, we feel you'll have an invaluable aid to a happier life.

■ ABOUT THE AUTHORS

Jose Stevens, PhD, is a writer and licensed psychotherapist in Berkeley, California. He obtained his masters degree in Social Work at the University of California at Berkeley and his doctorate in Integral Counseling at the California Institute of Integral Studies in San Francisco. He has been on the faculty at John F. Kennedy University since 1980, has appeared on CBS "People Are Talking," and is a frequent guest on television and radio. As the author and co-author of five books and numerous articles, he has traveled both nationally and internationally, teaching and lecturing on essence and personality, the use of intuition, and developing personal power through shamanism. For information regarding workshops, consultation, and training write to P.O. Box 5314, Berkeley, California, 94705.

JP Van Hulle is a well-known Bay Area author, teacher, and consultant. A California native, she graduated from U. C. Berkeley and ran a sanctuary program for Oakland's homeless. For the next few years, she taught courses in communication and sexuality at the Institute of Human Abilities in Oakland, CA. She instituted a non-profit organization to support underprivileged children and provided educational retraining for disabled adults, battered women, and victims of incest and physical abuse. She has traveled extensively throughout the U. S. lecturing on essence and personality, doing private consultations, and making audio and video educational tapes. She has been developing, testing, and working with personality systems since 1982. This is her fourth book on personality systems and two more are in process. For information regarding classes, consultations, tapes or literature write to P. O. Box 675, Orinda, CA 94563.

■ PERSONALITY PUZZLE

To order additional copies of the E.P.P. test
(The Essence and Personality Profile):

	Item Amount	Shipping & Handling
Packet of 5 E.P.P.'s	$16.25	$2.50
Packet of 25 E P.P.'s	$75.00	$3.50
Packet of 100 E.P.P.'s	$300.00	$6.00
Subtotal	$_____	
California Sales Tax 7.25% (Or Resale Number)	$_____	
Shipping & Handling Subtotal		$_____
TOTAL	$_____	

Please make checks payable to:
        Affinity Press
        P. O. Box 675
        Orinda, CA 94563

If you would like to order less than 5 copies of the E.P.P. please
make your check payable to Rainbow Collective, same address.
Include $3.25 each, plus $1.00 shipping & handling. Calif.
residents please add 7.25% sales tax.